HAPPINESS INDEED

HAPPINESS INDEED

AN ACTOR'S LIFE

Denis Quilley

OBERON BOOKS

LONDON

First published in 2004 by Oberon Books Ltd.
(incorporating Absolute Classics)
521 Caledonian Road, London N7 9RH
Tel: 020 7607 3637 / Fax: 020 7607 3629
e-mail: oberon.books@btinternet.com
www.oberonbooks.com

A catalogue record for this book is available from the British Library.

ISBN: 1 84002 268 X

Cover design: Jon Morgan

Every effort has been made to trace the photographers of all pictures reprinted in this book. Acknowledgement is made in all cases where photographer and/or source is known.

Proofread by Prufrock – www.prufrock.co.uk

Printed in Great Britain by Antony Rowe Ltd, Chippenham

Contents

The first set of photographs (pages I–XVI) are to be found between pages 88 and 89; the second set (pages XVII–XXXII) between pages 168 and 169.

Acknowledgements

Thanks are due to the following for their much appreciated help and contributions: Sophie Baker; Michael Blakemore; Christopher Fry; Lyn Haill; Nottingham Archive; Open Air Theatre, Regent's Park; Sarah Pond; Pam Remnant; Royal National Theatre Archives; John Timbers; Anthony and Susan Valentine.

Photographs are reproduced by kind permission of the following copyright holders: Catherine Ashmore/Dominic Photography; Sophie Baker; Clive Barda/ArenaPAL; Clive Capstick/Rex; Nobby Clark; Anthony Crickmay; Donald Cooper; Robert Day; Zoe Dominic/ Dominic Photography; John Haynes; Ivan Kyncl; *Manchester Evening News*; Brian Moody/Scope; Alastair Muir; David Sim; The Theatre Museum, V&A; John Timbers; Susan Valentine; Reg White/Rex; Reg Wilson.

FOREWORD
by Sir Peter Hall

THE OUTSIDE WORLD often thinks of actors as self-obsessed creatures. But they are not – particularly in the theatre, where every performer is dependent on his fellows. Denis Quilley was a leading player who yet always cared for the team; a shining personality who always put the play before himself. We can take his great and versatile talent – as actor, singer and performer – as read; above all we must celebrate his kindness, his generosity (particularly to beginners) and his unfailing support of others in the cause of the profession he loved. He was a remarkable man.

I have bedimm'd
The noontide sun, call'd forth the mutinous winds,
And 'twixt the green sea and the azur'd vault
Set roaring war: to the dread-rattling thunder
Have I given fire, and rifted Jove's stout oak
With his own bolt: the strong-based promontory
Have I made shake; and by the spurs pluck'd up
The pine and cedar: graves at my command
Have waked their sleepers, oped, and let 'em forth
By my so potent art. But this rough magic
I here abjure.

WILLIAM SHAKESPEARE

No man is an island, entire of itself; every man is a piece of the
Continent, a part of the main... Any man's death diminishes me,
because I am involved in Mankind; and therefore never send to know
for whom the bell tolls: it tolls for thee.

JOHN DONNE

Preamble

BREAKFAST TIME on St Valentine's Day, and Stella and I are dancing sedately but quite stylishly round the kitchen while Frank Sinatra's voice, that devastating blend of cocky street-wise cool and little-boy-lost vulnerability, fills the air with wit and warmth, dazzling musical improvisation and spontaneously perfect phrasing. To suit the occasion he's singing 'My Funny Valentine' – written by Rodgers and Hart for a girl to sing, but hijacked by Frank and his hit-man Nelson Riddle, and now theirs by right and forever.

Last night Pavarotti had woven a different magic. It was our son's twenty-seventh birthday dinner in the local trattoria, and as we all ate minestrone and spaghetti Big Lucy sang Verdi and Puccini and Neapolitan folk songs in a voice overflowing with Mediterranean sunshine, chianti and the open air.

Happiness is notoriously difficult to define and even more difficult to achieve. Chasing it is a waste of time – The Pursuit of Happiness as enshrined in The American Dream is surely a chimera. Pleasure can be pursued and found, so can comfort and wealth and prestige, but happiness sneaks up on you unbidden and unexpected, like a child putting his hand in yours.

I was very happy that Valentine's Day morning.

I have never kept diaries and my memory is as fallible as the next man's, so what follows may sometimes be coloured too rosy by nostalgia and sentiment, and may well put some events in the wrong order or the wrong place.

Perhaps, though, there is some virtue in my imperfect recall.

Montaigne famously said: 'Unless a man feels he has a good enough memory he should never venture to lie.'

Small danger of that, at least.

Chapter 1
Auntie Amy's Kitchen

IT'S 1977, and I'm waiting to make my entrance in the first performance of Peter Nichols' *Privates on Parade* at the Aldwych theatre in London. I'm playing Acting Captain Terri Dennis, a slightly over-the-hill drag queen who's running an Army Entertainments Unit in Malaysia. As my first entrance is through the auditorium and up on to the stage, I'm waiting, not in the wings, but by the door leading from the foyer to the stalls. A late-arriving couple squeeze past me to their seats, raising their eyebrows and obviously wondering what this vision with the mascara, the blue-rinsed temples and the dinky little pink scarf knotted round his neck is doing cruising the corridors of a West End theatre.

Already up on stage playing a foul-mouthed corporal is Joe Melia, with whom I have been anxiously discussing the show's chances just before curtain up. It has, after all, a lot of bad language, some absolutely filthy jokes and a lot of explicit gay ones – will it offend the squeamish and fall flat on its face or will it take off and fly? And will they find my second-rate old female impersonator touching and endearing or crude and unfunny? Well, let's see. In I go through the audience, their heads turning in surprise; Joe shouts in a toe-curling Brummy accent: 'Where you fookin' bin, Terri? We bin fookin' waitin' for you!' With an icy hauteur worthy of Bette Davis I draw myself up to my full height and reply: 'You *dare* speak to an officer like that and I'll scream the place down!' There is a huge warm laugh and Joe gives me a slow wink with his upstage eye which says: 'I think we're going to be all right, guvnor.' A wave of relief and happiness engulfs me, and I am transported back forty years to Auntie Amy's Kitchen.

She must have had other rooms – a living room, bedrooms, a bathroom – but I don't remember them. The kitchen was where the action was. A long low basement room with a black iron coal-burning cooking-range right across one end and a long, long table running lengthways down the middle. It was lit by gas: handsome rise-and-fall fitments that you pulled down from the ceiling before putting a match to the delicate tracery of the mantle, which popped softly as it ignited, then returned smoothly to the ceiling at a gentle touch from your fingertips.

There were mysterious regions up above, where Miss Brown was rumoured to live, but I never saw her; I never even ventured up those broad Axminster-carpeted stairs. They had an alien smell, a forbidding upholstered opulence and a silence quite at odds with the crowded, noisy, warm, laughing, singing, loving room down below.

On special occasions of any kind – Christmas, birthdays, weddings, anniversaries – this was where everyone gathered: my father Cliff and his nine brothers and sisters, and the seven Stanleys (they used to boast that they were related to Lord Derby) my mother Ada, and Amy, Edie, Emmie, Lizzie, Polly, and poor uncle Walter, the only boy and the inevitable butt of all their merciless anti-male jokes. Perhaps as a revolt against all those jolly, plump, robust Cockney girls, he married my auntie Lil, a slim rather elegant lady who spoke with an accent more refined than any I had heard before, and drank gin and It rather than the port and lemon which was the usual tipple of the Stanley girls.

With all these aunts and uncles, of course, I had more cousins than I could count – little girls in their best dresses who were nice to me but altogether too exotic for me to engage in witty conversation, and big boys whom I shyly revered and envied – sharp, confident, Brylcreemed lads in breathtakingly wonderful electric blue double-breasted suits with white art-silk scarves precisely folded and tucked round their necks inside their jackets so that half an inch of white showed in the vee of their magnificently wide and pointed lapels.

Cousin Connie was always in charge of the proceedings. She made sure everyone had pencils and paper for the word games; she would find a bed-sheet for two of the boys to hold up while I cranked the handle of the film projector I had been given for Christmas, sending faint black and white images of Felix the Cat flickering across the room; she would supervise the laying of the long table for high tea; but most important of all, she would organise the Turns.

This was what made these family gatherings into something which still resonates in my heart more than half a century later: everybody – absolutely everybody – had to do a Turn. Dad and uncle Dick Turpin (who was not really an uncle but an old friend of the family elevated to honorary uncle status) would sing 'The Two Gendarmes': 'We run them in, we run them in'. Mum would play the piano (Lehar's 'Gold and Silver' waltz was always a firm favourite) and perhaps sing a duet with auntie Edie; my sister Paddy and cousin Joyce, who lived next door to us and was really a second sister to me, might be persuaded to recite a poem; one of the boys would probably do a tap-dance and one of the uncles would come up with a humorous monologue – 'Albert and the Lion,' maybe, or 'Sam, Sam, pick up thy musket' – and then the moment of heart-stopping terror when a cowboy hat was put on my head and I stepped out in my short trousers and Just William socks in front of that talented, brilliantly dressed and discerning audience to sing 'Old faithful, we roam the range together' in my untutored boyish treble.

They seemed to enjoy it – one or two of the boys joined in the last couple of lines:

When your round-up days are over
There'll be pastures full of clover
For you, old faithful pal of mine

and then the fearful but exhilarating responsibility was over, and I could relax and enjoy myself while the whole room sang together.

A lifetime later, an old ham of ripe vintage and vast experience, each time I step on stage for the first time in a new production, be it at Drury Lane, the Palladium or my second home the National Theatre, I am still that little boy in short trousers trying not to panic, and hoping desperately that my huge extended family out there in the dark will welcome me and enjoy themselves as much as they did in Auntie Amy's Kitchen.

She lived in Islington in north London long, long before gentrification brought restaurants with names like Granita and residents with names like Tony Blair. Her husband, uncle Tom, worked for a firm of scientific instrument makers called Negretti and Zambra, but we weren't allowed to tell our friends this when the war started, because the Italians were on the wrong side. We played in the street as all children did then, and were allowed to venture through 'The Hole in the Wall,' an archway leading to Almeida Street, a quiet little cul-de-sac now globally renowned for enticing the likes of Kevin Spacey and Cate Blanchett to the phenomenally successful Almeida Theatre.

Our own home was just round the corner in two rooms at the top of a tall house in Tyndale Terrace. All I remember is a big square yellowish porcelain sink on the landing below with a cold tap at which my mother filled buckets to take upstairs. On Mondays lots of extra buckets went up and were poured into the copper, a great shining kettle-drum with a gas-ring under it, to be heated up for the weekly wash.

We eventually left Tyndale Terrace to live in Ilford, but the gatherings in Islington continued with unabated regularity and undiminished delight. I found suburban respectability a poor substitute for grimy inner-city street life, but when my mother first walked into the new house (a very ordinary pebble-dashed end-of-terrace semi) she sighed, 'Oh, Cliff, it's so beautiful,' and burst into tears.

Well, it wasn't very beautiful but it did have a little front garden and a living room that went through from front to back, with French windows opening on to a strip of concrete and thence to a sizeable back garden where my father was at last able to indulge his passion for growing things: a few flowers, some rambling roses along the fence, but his real treasures were the tomatoes, carrots, potatoes and parsnips, and the jewel in the crown was the apple tree (James Grieve). He had a life-long dream of retiring to a little cottage with a plot of land – 'an acre, son, just an acre' where he could happily dig and sow and harvest, and come home to drink tea, sing hymns and watch the sun go down. He never achieved it. During the war he did the next best thing and got an allotment just a short bicycle ride from home, but this, although it gave him great joy, was really taken on as a patriotic duty; he was already in the Home Guard, armed with a pick-handle which stood in the umbrella stand in the hall in case a German paratrooper should land in the front garden, and when we were exhorted to 'Dig for Victory,' that's what he did.

He was a very good man – a real Christian with a profound love and respect for his fellow man. Honour and Duty were his watchwords, and he never betrayed them. His formal education was fairly basic. Like me, he tried for a scholarship to a good secondary school, but unlike me he missed the tram that would have got him to the exam in good time, and ran all the way there, arriving in a panic, sweating and exhausted, and quite unable to compose himself for the ordeal that faced him. But he had a good brain and an inquiring disposition, and like many of his generation he educated himself through the public library, evening classes and dogged determination. He discovered a passion for Dickens, and saved up to buy a complete edition, uniformly bound and with its own glass-fronted bookcase. He read every one of them from cover to cover.

He also discovered a gift for healing, which nowadays would have given him quite a social cachet, but was in those days considered rather eccentric and dotty. If I had a pain – a bruised or cut knee, say, as a result of some over-enthusiastic street game – he would place his hands on it saying 'Empty your mind, son, think of something happy. Oh yes, I can feel it now, it's coming through my hands and up my arm. It's going, it's going – it's gone.' And it would be gone. If I couldn't sleep at night he would put a hand on my forehead and tell me to close my eyes and picture a blue sky with soft white clouds moving slowly and quietly across it, and pretty soon I was asleep. Of course my unquestioning faith in him made me an ideally suggestible subject, but it was a genuine gift, and he used it to help sceptics as well as believers.

In the First World War he was wounded in the leg, and taken by stretcher to a Field Hospital (an impressive-sounding name for a tent in the mud) where he was laid out at the end of a line of wounded all waiting their turn. There was one officer doing the operations, and a sergeant armed with bottles of chloroform was the rough-and-ready anaesthetist. By the time his turn finally came he was racked with pain, and shaking with fear after seeing and hearing what the men ahead of him had endured. When the chloroform-soaked pad was slapped over his nose and mouth he fought tooth and nail to avoid going under, terrified that he would not come back again. His last memory was of the sergeant saying: 'I can't get this bugger out, Sir,' and the officer replying: 'Well, whack some more bloody chloroform on him, man.' The sergeant smashed the top off a new bottle, the pad hit him again, and he was out.

Many years later, when I was a teenager, he suffered a hernia, which grew steadily worse until I said:

'You know, Dad, you really must go into hospital and get that hernia fixed.'

'I'm not going into hospital, Son – I've been there, I know what it's like.'

'But you *don't* know what it's like, Dad – this isn't the Somme, it wouldn't be like that at all, it's –'

'Son, I'm *not* going into hospital, and that's *that*.'

Soon afterwards, the hernia strangulated, and he was whisked into hospital in the early hours of the morning and operated on later that day. I went to see him in the evening.

'How was it, Dad?'

'Oh, Son, if only I'd known.'

'What do you mean?'

'Well, I had a nice chat with the young lady, then she put a needle in my arm and I had a bit of a doze, and when I woke up I said, "When are you going to do it?" and she said, "We've done it, dear, we've done it." Oh, Son – if only I'd known!'

In case I seem to be painting a picture of someone otherworldly and ineffectual, let me say at once that he was the most practical and competent of men. Like my son (but most assuredly not like me), he could do anything with his hands and the right tools. Everything that needed doing in the house he did single-handed: painting and decorating, plastering, carpentry, plumbing, electrics, brick-laying – he repaired all our shoes on a big iron last with four different-sized feet, cutting the leather for the soles, taking a mouthful of nails and banging them in with a big flat rasp.

After leaving school to be a telegram delivery boy (smart uniform with pill-box hat and always salute when the lady or gentleman opens the door) he soon became a fully-fledged telegraphist in the Central Telegraph Office, sending telegrams by Morse code. During the war he was moved to Bletchley and was away from home for weeks at a time. He never said why he was sent there or what he was doing – only that his office had been moved to Bletchley. It was not until years after the war was over that we learned he had been part of the great Enigma code-breaking team. He had signed the Official Secrets Act and, honest and conscientious as ever, never gave a hint what he was up to. Even my mother hadn't known.

He met her when they were both singing in the choir of St Silas' church in Highbury. They both had untrained but naturally sweet singing voices, and my mother was quite an accomplished pianist. In the new house in Ilford there was room for an upright piano, and every week she would buy *Popular Music* (3d every Thursday, edited by Henry Hall, leader of the BBC Dance Orchestra) which contained four or five of the most popular songs of the day – a sort of sheet-music Top of the Pops – and every week the four of us, Mum and Dad, Paddy and I, would sing through them all: 'Old Father Thames,' 'Sleepy Lagoon,' and Gracie Fields' latest hit 'The Isle of Capri,' which began with the spine-tingling anticipation of ''Twas on the Isle of Capri that I met her' and ended with the tragic desolation of 'She wore a plain golden ring on her finger – 'twas goodbye to the Isle of Capri'. The Osmonds we were not, but we made a merry noise.

One good thing about Ilford was that it was near Woodford. This, I hear you say, is a poor recommendation. Stay with me – I am serious. When I was ten and a bit, my primary school headmaster prevailed upon my surprised and delighted parents to take me on a visit to Drapers Hall. This was, and is, a building of some splendour in Throgmorton Street in the City of London. Great curving staircases led up to high-ceilinged, nobly proportioned and richly furnished rooms. In one of those rooms there were fifty or so ordinary school desks, for this was the home of the Drapers Company, who each year endowed three Boarding Foundation Scholarships to Bancroft's School in Woodford Green in Essex, and the reason why this over-awed boy and his even more over-awed father were setting foot so deferentially in this ancient and honourable establishment was that I had been chosen to sit the examination to qualify for one of those greatly sought-after scholarships.

I sat the exam, I won the scholarship, I went to Bancroft's, and my life changed.

From the road skirting Woodford Green, a gravel drive led to a handsome two-storey red-brick neo-Elizabethan façade with an imposing twin-turreted tower in the centre. Under the tower was an archway big enough for a sizeable coach and horses to drive through, and in the archway was the snug little cubby-hole where George the porter held sway. Nobody went in or out without George's knowledge and consent, and our arrival on my first day was duly noted and assessed: I think the fact that I was to be one of the hundred boarders rather than one of the three hundred day-boys slightly raised my status in George's estimation, compensating for our distinctly unworldly and lower-middle-class appearance. Once accepted by George and ticked off on his list, we passed through the archway and emerged into a beautiful quadrangle surrounded on two sides by cloisters, on the third side by a chapel with a gorgeous Gothic stained-glass window, and open on the far side to a flight of stone steps and a grassy embankment which led to a huge green playing-field. Two rugby pitches at one end, a cricket square in the middle, a pavilion at the other end, a running track round the perimeter, and at the farthest boundary the ancient beech trees of Epping Forest.

I never went to university, much to my parents' disappointment, but from visiting friends and contemporaries who did, and from teaching English and American drama students at Oxford colleges, I know the feel, the ambience of university life, and with hindsight I can see that Bancroft's offered me the nearest approximation to that experience that one could have without actually going there.

Everything, of course, was not perfect. My Maths teacher, for example, was a sarcastic sadist who once, catching my expression of distaste at whatever it was that he was saying or doing in class that day, said: 'You look as if you'd like to hit me, Quilley – why don't you then?' So I punched him in the solar plexus. As thirty boys had heard his invitation, he was not in a strong position to complain. Chemistry was in the hands of a sweetly eccentric old boy with an unidentifiable rural accent whose brain worked according to a completely different set of rules from mine. On the innumerable occasions when the only honest answer I could give to one of his incomprehensible questions was, 'I don't know, sir,' back would come, with reassuring inevitability, the refrain, 'I do not know, I cannot tell, my ignorance is terri-bell!' It would come out with the same new-minted freshness on the nineteenth occasion as on the first – rather like those sergeant-majors who *all* say: 'Am I hurting you, lad?' 'No, sir.' 'Well I should be – I'm standing on your effing hair –

get it CUT!' and seem rather touchingly, to think that you really believe they have brilliantly made it up on the spur of the moment.

The man who taught me English and Latin had no need of such psychological crutches. Don Francombe would wander across the quadrangle to his classroom in his patched old tweed jacket, his black university gown faded to a rather chic grey-green, wreathed in pipe-smoke and carrying with him a dreamy, genial air of detached contentment.

I liked him at once, and formed a rapport with him which ripened into a friendship which has lasted to this day. The last part he saw me play at the National Theatre was Falstaff in *The Merry Wives of Windsor*, in 1995. On the way home he treated his son to a long and erudite dissertation on the nature of Shakespearean comedy and the difference between the Falstaff of *Henry IV* and the much less complex character in *The Merry Wives*. For fifty years he had managed to see practically everything I ever did in the theatre, and always buoyed me up with his enthusiasm and pride and his wise, discerning criticism.

As well as teaching me English and Latin, he also ran the school choir and directed all the school plays. But he did far more than that: he opened the golden doors of perception, and led me into a brave and magical new world – a world inhabited by Shakespeare, Keats and Milton, by Mozart, Brahms and Debussy, by John Gielgud, Peggy Ashcroft and Laurence Olivier. He achieved this not by formal tuition – he was the least didactic of teachers, and not much of a disciplinarian – but by creating an ambience in which those of us who wanted to could absorb, almost without realising it, his gentle but firmly-held view of the world, its inhabitants and their achievements. The Greek and Roman classics were the bedrock of Western civilisation; Chaucer, Shakespeare and Pope were the natural fruit of the great tree so firmly planted by Homer, Aeschylus, Cicero and Virgil. In the same way Haydn, Mozart and Beethoven led music inevitably, via Brahms, into the nineteenth-century Romantic tradition.

Needless to say, I didn't absorb all this in one fell swoop – it was a gradual journey of discovery which spanned seven years and has continued ever since. It began when I joined the Music Club and found that there were pieces of music which lasted longer than one side of a 10-inch 78rpm gramophone record. My childhood had been full of music, of course, but this was music of an altogether different order – something which I knew I had to grapple with seriously in order to understand its structure and its intellectual and emotional meaning, but which I also knew would repay the effort many times over. I joined the choir and under Don's guidance we were performing works like Britten's *Ceremony of Carols* and Brahms' *German Requiem* when other choirs were trudging through the likes of Stainer's *Crucifixion*. I sang the solos, first as a treble then as a baritone, and we made some very good music; when the choir joined forces with the local girls' school they were chosen by Herbert von Karajan to be the children's chorus in his recording of the opera *Hansel and Gretel*.

Alongside this white-knuckle roller-coaster ride into the world of real music another dizzying journey was taking me from the foothills up to the Himalayan peaks of the theatre. Before I was born, my parents used to go to their local theatre, Collins Music Hall, usually sitting either in the Upper Circle or the Pit, which was the last half-dozen rows of the Stalls, tucked under the Dress Circle, not too good for seeing or hearing and priced accordingly (unlike today, when they are called Orchestra Stalls all the way to the back wall and priced accordingly). Occasionally, when Mum and Dad were feeling flush, they would venture into the stalls, which were ennobled with the wonderful title of Fauteuils – 'armchairs' if you looked them up in the French dictionary, but universally known to the Islington locals as the Futicles. On one memorable occasion they were watching a Victorian melodrama (I think it was *Maria Marten – Murder in the Red Barn*) and at the climactic moment when the villain had the heroine tied up and was just preparing to subject her to some unspeakable fate almost certainly worse than death, a young lady in the Futicle next to them jumped to her feet in tears and shouted 'You wicked old sod!' Oh, for such total and unselfconscious involvement from a present-day TV-sated audience!

Nothing quite so delightful ever happened during my youthful visits to the theatre, but with cousin Connie we went to pantomimes at Christmas, we saw Jean Forbes-Robertson in *Peter Pan* and Anton Dolin in *Where the Rainbow Ends*, and hugely enjoyed Joe Loss's Dance Band and Billy ('almost a gentleman') Bennett topping the bill at the Ilford Hippodrome. But then, in my first year at Bancroft's I saw some of the older boys (the grandly-named Bancroft's Players) in *As You Like It*, and the giant Shakespeare with his gorgeous language, earthy wit and humane philosophy, barged roughly and unstoppably into my life.

Rosalind was played by a boy who went on to be a professor of Oriental languages. Impossible at this distance to guess how good he was, but quite certainly his diction was clear and beautiful, he moved with grace, he was playfully and movingly feminine without being in the least effeminate. I think my enraptured response must have been very like that of the groundlings who first saw Rosalind played by a boy of much the same age at the Globe four hundred years ago. I was instantly overwhelmed, and determined to be part of this beautiful, uplifting and dangerous existence.

I joined the Bancroft's Players, and my first ever acting role was Sir Hugh Evans in the *Merry Wives of Windsor*. Our French teacher

17

was a perky little Welshman called Ivor Jenkins, who was also a nimble performer on the double-bass and was often called upon when the school orchestra needed reinforcement in the nether regions. His accent was lilting and musical, his body language energetic and expansive, and I based my Hugh Evans firmly on him, to the great delight of my schoolmates who recognised him with gratifying ease. At our French lesson the next day he said:

'Well, Quilley, I must admit you have got me down to a T.'

My first rave review!

'Thank you, Sir, thank you very much.'

'Yes, well, more important matters – "Le Corbeau et le Renard".'

The wit and irony of La Fontaine's elegant little fable about the crow and the fox received only half my attention that morning. I was still reliving the pleasure of last night's performance and looking forward to the next one this evening. I was beginning to realise that I might have found what I really wanted to do.

I was not a bad all-rounder at school: very good at some things, averagely competent at others, and utterly useless at Chemistry and Physics. I was a prefect (my fag, a very bright lad called Fred Emery, became Washington correspondent of *The Times* and an influential political commentator on television). I was in the Gymnastics team and the Rugby First XV, so all in all I was extremely happy and fulfilled, with lots of friends, and constantly stimulated and challenged.

But the moment I stepped on to a stage I knew this was my métier. I was frightened and yet totally at home, and I knew instinctively what to do, just as other boys seemed to know instinctively how to put together those strange and intimidating pieces of glass and rubber in the Chemistry lab, make them into a fearsome and efficient machine and perform the scientific experiment whose basic premise

I could not begin to understand. When we read plays in class with Don Francombe – or even Racine and Corneille in French with Ivor Jenkins – I knew where to place an emphasis, where to pause, where to speed up or slow down, and where the emotional climaxes were. I was as baffled by the inability of some of my friends to do the same as they no doubt were by my total incompetence with pipettes and Bunsen burners.

I progressed from Sir Hugh Evans to the Handsome Captain (type-casting already) in Shaw's *Androcles and the Lion*, Richard II in Gordon Daviot's *Richard of Bordeaux* (the play which launched John Gielgud as a West End star) and Caesar in Shaw's *Caesar and Cleopatra*. Many years later, after a performance at the Old Vic with the National Theatre, my dresser ushered in a very tall, bearded young man whom I didn't recognise at all. He grinned down at me from a great height, grasped my hand in his huge paw and said in a deep bass voice, 'Hallo! You won't remember me – I'm Jim Nursaw and I played Cleopatra to your Caesar at Bancroft's School.' Well, he had changed a bit. Sir James Nursaw is now Legal Advisor to the House of Lords.

By the time I was seventeen and into my last year at school it was absolutely clear that the theatre was where I was going to earn my living and that music, one way or another, would have an equally important place in the scheme of things. A few defining experiences made the decision for me, simply and irrevocably.

I used to go regularly to the Proms at the Albert Hall in the summer holidays, queuing up for the two-shilling standing places in the arena. If you were early in the queue you got to the front, which meant that you had a rail to lean on to take a bit of weight off your feet, and also that you were really close to the orchestra, and even closer to the soloist. One evening Anthony Pini was playing the Elgar Cello

Concerto, which I was hearing for the first time. He played the first two movements exquisitely but boldly, with great panache and projection, then he closed his eyes, composed himself and began the slow movement, the tone this time still rich and warm but veiled and muted. After a minute or so, tears began to creep gently out from under his closed eyelids and run slowly down his cheeks. Joy and sadness lit up his face simultaneously, inseparably; he was a vessel, a conduit through which a divine message (from Elgar? from God? who knows?) was being handed down.

The tears flowed until the movement came to its hushed and wondering end, and here is the marvellous thing: all that time his technique never faltered for an instant. The bowing was firm and relaxed, the fingering was confident and precise, with every note perfectly in tune, the phrasing so natural and inevitable that there was no need to open his eyes to see the conductor's beat – they just breathed it together.

I was standing, transfixed, perhaps ten feet away from this magical event, and it remains the most amazing demonstration I ever saw of the way in which a great interpretative artist can totally submit himself to the emotional demands of a great work of art while at the same time keeping a rigorous third eye on the physical nuts and bolts of performance, and a third ear constantly aware of the audience's reaction. On the rare occasions when I manage to achieve something remotely comparable, I mentally spool back – Albert Hall, summer of 1945 – and say, 'Thank you, Mr Pini.'

There are some things which, although they are constantly changing in small details – in the way they are presented to you, or in little day-to-day variations in their shape or condition – nevertheless remain always essentially the same. They have a strong and individual inner life which nothing can destroy. These are the things of which one never tires – bread, wine, the sea, Mozart's *Marriage of Figaro*, Shakespeare's *Hamlet*.

Hamlet was just one of the many texts we studied for our Higher School Certificate that year – not surprisingly, it was the one that interested me most. We examined its structure, worked out why some of it was in verse and some in prose, argued about various line-readings. I found it endlessly fascinating, but intricate and difficult. I thought I knew it well – until I saw it acted. Don Francombe took half a dozen of us to the Haymarket Theatre to see John Gielgud play it, and the difficulties dissolved into thin air. The lightness, speed and fluidity of his delivery simply admitted no possibility of problems of any kind. The meaning was crystal clear, the shape of the verse meticulously observed, but easily and naturally, without any over-emphasis. The character and the play sprang elegantly and movingly to life, and from then on my dog-eared school copy (which I still have) was no longer an academic textbook but a repository of dreams. Like a prosaic-looking musical box which plays an enchanting tune when you lift its lid, I had only to open the battered cover (*Hamlet*, edited by A W Verity MA – property of D C Quilley, form VI B, Arts) for my eyes and ears to be ravished by the sights and sounds of this most profound and disturbingly beautiful of all dramatic poems.

Peter Grimes was a revelation of a different sort – perhaps even more powerful because I had no idea of the shock that was in store for me. Benjamin Britten's opera burst on to London's musical scene in 1945 with much the sort of impact which John Osborne's *Look Back in Anger* made on the theatrical scene in 1956. In each case a major new talent was flinging down his calling-card, saying, 'This is me – here I am!' just as Brahms did with his First Symphony in 1876. We took the number 38 bus from Woodford Green to Islington; as we rode up Rosebery Avenue and approached the bus-stop outside Sadler's Wells Theatre the bus-conductor called out: 'All off here for the singing fisherman.' So off we all got, and oh – how the fisherman sang!

My acquaintance with opera was almost non-existent: I had seen *The Bartered Bride* and greatly enjoyed its jolly tunes and rustic dances, and I had heard some popular arias on gramophone records, but nothing had prepared me for the visceral impact of this story of the misfit East Anglian fisherman who abused his boy apprentices while yearning hopelessly for the love of Ellen Orford, the village school-teacher, and ended his life by sinking his fishing boat in the North Sea.

The story itself was engrossing enough, but Britten's music brought to it a whole new dimension of terror and beauty. Firmly rooted in tonality, brushing aside Schoenberg's arbitrary, arid and mechanical systems of atonality and 'tone-rows,' and yet all the time pushing traditional tonality to the limits of possibility, this music spoke directly to open-hearted seventeen-year-olds in a language that we instinctively understood.

From the very opening bars, evoking the big skies and cold beaches of Suffolk, through moonlight and storm and drunken gaiety to the final, inevitable disaster, and on into the coda, with its Shakespearean acceptance that after every human tragedy life goes on very much as before, this was music that in every bar understood, enhanced and illuminated the meaning of the words. This surely was what the Italian composers of the seventeenth and eighteenth centuries meant when they talked of *Dramma per Musica* – the perfect fusion of words and music.

My poor dear parents were devastated when I told them I wanted to become a professional actor. They had been so proud when I won the scholarship, and equally proud of my reasonably good academic progress, and they assumed I was heading for a university degree and either an academic career or something really respectable like a high-up post in the Civil Service. They were bitterly disappointed at what they saw as the waste of a good education, but once they saw that I was deadly serious they graciously went along with me, and later, when I started to do well in the profession, I am happy to think that I made them proud again.

Don Francombe asked around all his friends and acquaintances to find out which was considered to be the best of the provincial repertory theatres (this, of course, was the Jurassic or pre-television era, when every town of any size boasted a Rep). The consensus of opinion was that Birmingham was Best, so that was where we would try for. We were aiming perilously high, for this was one of the most famous and distinguished theatres in the country, where legends like Laurence Olivier and Ralph Richardson had cut their teeth. Undaunted, Don and I between us composed a letter to the Artistic Director, Sir Barry Jackson, asking for an audition, and to our amazement a very prompt reply from the great man suggested an early date for an audition, and commanded me to prepare three pieces, including one of Hamlet's soliloquies, one of the Chorus speeches from *Henry V*, and a piece of my own choosing. I frantically learned Hamlet's 'O what a rogue and peasant slave am I' and Chorus's 'Now entertain conjecture of a time / When creeping murmur and the poring dark / Fills the wide vessel of the universe,' and Don coached me intensively through them both, plus a speech from Ibsen's *Peer Gynt* which I already knew. He somehow persuaded the headmaster to give me a day off school, Mum and Dad bought me a return ticket to Birmingham, the appointed day arrived and off I went, petrified.

I found the Rep with the aid of my A–Z street map. That took me about thirty seconds as it was right next door to New Street Station, in (wait for it) Station Street – not by any means the most beautiful or salubrious thoroughfare in the Second City. The next problem was how to get in. The front looked a bit closed and deserted and I wondered where the Stage Door might be, if indeed there was one – I had never been backstage in a theatre and was not well versed in these matters. I eventually found a dingy alley which seemed to be aiming towards the back of the building. I ventured down it, turned a corner, and there was the magic sign 'Stage Door'. I walked through the open door next to it and found myself surrounded by a dozen or so coffins in various stages of construction, none of them, to my intense relief, containing a corpse, as far as I could see. I had stumbled into the rough business end of an undertaker's establishment which had a very genteel frontage on Station Street a few yards along from the theatre. A burly shirt-sleeved lad in the dim far corner saw my dismay, sussed me out instantly and said, 'Next door, mate,' jerking his thumb the way I had just come.

And indeed, next door, right underneath the Stage Door sign was a small, drab, closed door much less inviting than its flashy neighbour. I knocked tentatively, turned the handle, and was greeted by a friendly sympathetic old chap who seemed to be expecting me, recognised my name when I gave it to him, told me what time I was supposed to do my bit, wished me luck and offered me a cup of tea, thereby igniting in me the first spark of a life-long love for all Stage Door keepers throughout the civilised world.

Someone fetched me and took me on to the stage. A cultured baritone from an invisible source in the darkened stalls said, 'Right, young Mr Quilley – let's see what you can do,' and I launched into my Three Pieces. I was semi-paralysed with fear, but I got through them without disaster. The voice said, 'Thank you Mr Quilley – just hang on a moment.' I hung on a moment, all right, and a tall, patrician gentleman (I use the word advisedly) smoking a cigarette in an elegant holder climbed on to the stage from the stalls and said: 'That was very good, Mr Quilley. I'd like to take you on as Assistant Stage Manager and general understudy.' I stood in dumb amazement rooted to the spot, goggling stupidly at Sir Barry (for it was he) until he said:

'When do you think you could st–'

'September, Sir.'

'Do you think you can live on four pounds a we–'

'Yes, Sir.'

I remember nothing more of that day. I obviously got myself back to London, and thence to Woodford and to bed. Next morning I told my mates, I rang up Mum and Dad on the payphone in the Tuck Shop and told them, I went to the Staff Common Room, knocked on the door and asked if I could speak to Mr Francombe, please. He came to the door preceded by a fragrant cloud of smoke from his ever-present pipe, I told him the news, and he said calmly in his soft Gloucestershire accent: 'Well done, Denis – I knew we'd make it.'

Chapter 2
In at the Deep End

A SMALL MAN (well, boy, really, he's hardly older than me) stands nervously but defiantly in a church hall in Birmingham addressing the assembled company. He is wearing a purple suit with a green shirt (which in 1945 is a major statement). He is twenty years old, just down from university, and Sir Barry Jackson has employed him to direct a season of plays at the Birmingham Rep including Shaw's *Man and Superman*, Shakespeare's *King John* and Ibsen's *The Lady from the Sea*.

'Right everyone,' he says with a great show of confidence and authority, 'We're doing *Man and Superman*, not Sir Barry's way but my way – that is, in period costumes and sets. Any questions?'

There is a silence, during which I can hear everyone thinking, 'Well, well, what have we got here then?' Eventually the leading man says, 'That seems sensible enough to me,' the others mumble agreement, and after a bit more chat, a look at the model of the set and the costume drawings, and some general discussion about hours of rehearsal and lunch breaks, everyone sits down and the first read-through of the play begins. An absolutely normal, mundane and unremarkable first day of rehearsals, except that the leading man is a handsome twenty-three-year-old Paul Scofield, one of the supporting roles is played by a boy of my age called Stanley Baker, who is understudied by another boy of my age called Paul Eddington, and the twenty-year-old in the purple suit who has been flung in at the deep end to tell these people how to do their job for the next three weeks is a promising young lad called Peter Brook. It is my very first day at work as Assistant Stage Manger, and I haven't the faintest idea what my duties are.

I had arrived in Birmingham a few days earlier in my best suit, and found my way to Handsworth Wood, a respectable suburb where Mrs Cox, a recently widowed lady with two grown-up daughters, lived in a large and pleasant house. By a great stroke of good fortune she was a friend of a friend of our family, and was very happy to rent me a room to bolster her meagre pension. She charged me thirty shillings a week for bed, breakfast and supper, and for an extra 2/6d she did my washing once a week. Most theatre digs in Birmingham at that time were £2 a week (really posh ones 3 guineas) so I was off to a flying start – my £4 a week was beginning to look quite handsome.

Birmingham was a Rolls-Royce among repertory theatres – most of the innumerable provincial Reps had to put on a new play every week. This is how it worked: let us suppose it is mid-season, the company has just finished playing *While Parents Sleep*, and the next two plays are *King Lear* and *Sailor Beware*. The weekly routine goes like this:

Monday night: opening performance of *Lear*

Tuesday morning and afternoon: read-through and set all the moves
    for *Sailor Beware*

Tuesday night: perform *Lear*

Wednesday morning: rehearse Act I of *Sailor Beware*

Wednesday afternoon: matinée of *Lear*

Wednesday night: *Lear* again

Thursday morning: rehearse Act II of *Sailor Beware*

Thursday afternoon: rehearse Act III of *Sailor Beware*

Thursday night: play *Lear*

Friday morning and afternoon: stagger through all of *Sailor Beware*

Friday night: play *Lear*

Saturday morning: straight run through of *Sailor Beware*

Saturday afternoon: matinée of *Lear*

Saturday night: last performance of *Lear*

Sunday: collapse in bed and have a last desperate look at the lines while the stage crew change the sets

Monday morning and afternoon: lighting and dress rehearsal of *Sailor Beware*

Monday night: opening performance of *Sailor Beware*

Tuesday morning: read-through *Lady Windermere's Fan*

and so on, and on.

You could be forgiven for thinking this the ultimate nightmare scenario, but hundreds of actors derived enormous pleasure and priceless experience from this gruelling but exciting regime, and loyal audiences all over the country had great fun seeing their favourites put on a different wig and a different accent each week.

By comparison our routine at Birmingham was positively luxurious: the average rehearsal period was three weeks, and for a major Shakespeare play or anything unusually long or complex, it could stretch to an unimaginably indulgent four weeks. Not only was I surrounded by an immensely talented group of people who between them could teach me everything I needed to know, but I was employed in a theatre which had probably the best working conditions and the highest artistic standards in the country. I had really fallen on my feet.

Watching Peter Brook trying to learn his craft as a director in the course of one short season was quite a revelation, and also quite a relief, because I knew that he was in exactly the same exciting but terrifying situation as I was: we were both pretending to know a lot more than we really did, playing it all by ear, making things up as we went along, and relying on instinct and native wit to see us through. He had a great gift for staging, for the use of music, for the orchestration of the look and the sound of a play, but he had no idea whatever how to give the actors meaningful direction as to how they should approach their roles or play their lines.

'That's not right,' he would say after a run-through of a scene.

'Well, what's wrong?' the actors would ask. 'What is it you want?'

'I don't know, but that's not it.'

After much trial and error the actors would be relieved to hear the youthful voice from the stalls cheerfully cry: 'That's it!'

Not surprisingly he knew nothing about the technicalities. At dress rehearsals Ted, the electrician, would be up his ladder shouting, 'What do you want in this lamp then, a 52 or a Straw, or what?'

'I don't know,' Peter would reply, 'I just want it more sort of pinkish over on the left.'

For my part it soon became clear that I was not cut out to be a stage manager. You need to be efficient and extremely well organised to be a good stage manager. You need a modicum of technical competence, plus the ability to stay calm and authoritative while nervous and hysterical actors are losing their heads all around you. You need to be able to improvise solutions to both mechanical and artistic crises in a split second, while still remembering to give all the right cues for music, lighting and stage crew. It is, in a word, a job for which I was not well qualified.

This did not worry me too much, since it was a job I did not really want. All the time I was being berated by Peter Brook for forgetting a crucial prop, for not being behind the fireplace with a cigarette lighter so that Paul Scofield could light a taper for his pipe, or for playing the wrong movement of Walton's *Façade* for the curtain-raiser to Act 3 of *Man and Superman*, my mind was on other things. Although excruciatingly and apologetically aware of the distress my incompetence must be causing everybody, I was actually only marking time until I could get out there on that stage and do what I had really come here to do – amaze the citizens of Birmingham with my brilliant dramatic skills and dazzle them with the irresistible force of my personality, while being paid real money for doing something I would cheerfully have done for nothing.

Fortunately Sir Barry, having put several promising teenagers on his payroll, came up with a play (an amusing American piece of fluff called *Spring Green*) which had good parts for four young boys. And so Stanley Baker (who went on to become Sir Stanley – film star and film producer), Alun Owen (who went on to become an award-winning playwright, author of *The Rough and Ready Lot* and countless TV dramas), Paul Eddington (who went on to become Prime Minister) and myself were all given an amazing chance to find our feet, spread our wings, and start the challenging and fascinating process of learning our craft.

None of us had been to Drama School – we learned on the job, which I am inclined to believe may be the best way. Of course Drama School can teach you all the essential peripheral skills (voice production, movement and so on) but despite the best efforts of Stanislavsky and his disciple Lee Strasberg, the central core, the *sine qua non* of acting cannot be taught. It is a gift, like a painter's eye or a musician's ear, which you are born with, and without it all the technical accomplishments which *can* be taught are of no avail.

You can learn how to mix pigments, how to stretch a canvas, how to render perspective correctly, but without the inspired vision which enabled Cézanne to make us see trees in a landscape through entirely different eyes, or Rembrandt to turn a straightforward self-portrait into a profound examination of the human predicament, you will never be a great painter. I can learn how to lay out a piece of piano music so that it lies gratefully for two or four hands, how to orchestrate, how to write for different types of voice so that the notes are comfortably within their range, but without Mozart's divine gift of plucking a melody out of the air and, by some strange alchemy, transforming a simple descending scale for Tamino in *The Magic Flute* into a golden celebration of wonder and love, I will never be a great composer.

I do not for a moment presume to elevate the actor's art to these Olympian heights – the great writers, composers, painters, sculptors, are all creators, while we are mere interpreters. And yet there is a gift – trivial perhaps, but at its best wonderful and magical – at the centre of it all. Some people can imagine that their mother has died and cry real tears, and some cannot; some people can think and feel themselves into the heart and brain of a Danish prince called Hamlet, whose uncle has killed his father and married his mother, and some cannot. It is an act of imagination, and of a particular type of imagination, probably most like that of a child at play who will whisper to you with total conviction: 'There's a lion behind that tree – let's see if we can catch him!' He knows quite well that you know there is no lion, but he also knows that if he imagines it intensely enough and expresses it truthfully enough, you will suspend your disbelief and go along with him. This is what we do every night.

It is enormously enjoyable, and has given me almost unalloyed pleasure for many years, but although I call us mere interpreters, I believe that in the highest reaches of the interpreter's art, true creativity comes into play. Olivier took the raw material that Shakespeare gave him in *Richard III* and created an enchanting, irresistible monster who was entirely faithful to Shakespeare's intention and yet somehow bigger, more dazzling and more horrible than you could imagine by looking at the words on the page. Maria Callas and Tito Gobbi grabbed hold of Sardou's story and Puccini's music and created a Floria Tosca and Baron Scarpia that Puccini could only have hoped for in his wildest dreams.

The great interpreters seem to be able to perform two apparently contradictory actions at the same time. On the one hand they project themselves (by that essential and mysterious act of imagination) into the heart and mind of a character entirely different from themselves, and adopt his physical, emotional and moral characteristics, and on the other hand they find some element in that character which they can identify with, which corresponds with something somewhere in their own psyche, and absorb that element back into themselves, mixing these disparate ingredients into something which, like the molecule of water which is made up of two atoms of hydrogen and one of oxygen, is greater than the sum of its parts.

(Perhaps my chemistry lessons were not a complete waste of time after all.)

Needless to say, my fledgling interpretative efforts were not quite in that league, but I did get better, and progressed from walk-ons to small parts to quite important parts, and was just beginning to gain confidence and feel I was really getting somewhere, when a buff envelope from the War Office plopped through the letter box of Mrs Cox's house and informed me that I was called up for National

Service. This was 1946 and the war was over, but conscription was still in force and I was just eighteen.

I went to rehearsal that morning very unhappily, taking the envelope with me to show my employers why they would shortly be obliged to dispense with my services, thereby nipping in the bud the blossoming career of the most brilliant talent ever to grace their stage (except, maybe, Olivier, Richardson, Margaret Leighton, Alan Badel, Albert Finney and a few others). As I walked into the rehearsal room, Stanley Baker stood there with an identical envelope in his big fist, and a look of complicity and commiseration in his eye. My spirits lifted a little – at least the two of us were in it together.

We did our basic training at Budbrook Barracks in Warwick, and after a week or two we were both given blue flashes to wear on the epaulettes of our battledress, which we were told signified 'Promising Soldier'. Whether that promise was ever fulfilled is a moot point (neither of us rose to dizzy heights). I am inclined to believe that the accolade was bestowed on us because we could spell Dog and Cat and add two and two. In my platoon of thirty men there were two for whom I used to read their letters from home and write their replies. They were very nice lads, and by no means unintelligent – they had just somehow slipped through the educational net, and they regarded my ability to read and write with awe and respect.

One of them asked me to give him lessons, which I instantly agreed to do. With only six weeks together, and not much spare time in the evenings after a brutal day of square-bashing, route-marches and weapon-training, we could not get very far, but in our last week I was absurdly moved when, at the beginning of a letter, most of which I had written for him, he wrote: 'Dear Mum, I wrote this bit myself' and at the end 'lots of love Mum from your loving son Jack.' I never saw him again and have no idea what happened to him, but I fervently hope that he persevered, and discovered the joy of reading and writing his glorious native language.

At the end of basic training I waved goodbye to Stanley Baker, who fetched up very cosily in Ditchling, in Sussex, and got on rather well with the village ladies. Various aptitude tests revealed, to no-one's surprise, that I had no mechanical gifts, but that I had a good ear and could distinguish one sound from another when they were played to me through earphones, and was therefore ideally suited to be a Wireless and Telegraph Operator in the Royal Corps of Signals, doing exactly what my father had done a generation before – sending messages by Morse Code.

I was to learn the mysteries of the trade in Catterick, a vast, bleak camp in Yorkshire which housed many different regiments learning many different skills under the supervision of a bunch of super-tough Regimental Sergeant Majors (the RSMs at Warwick were kindly uncles by comparison). Everything was organised with absolute mathematical precision: the length of sheet turned down over the blanket on your bed, the placing of the kit laid out on the bed for inspection, the position of the spare pair of boots by your bedside locker, all had to be accurate to the millimetre. Not a speck of dust was allowed anywhere, webbing belts and brasses had to be blancoed and polished to within an inch of their lives; the stone blocks surrounding the Nissen huts were whitewashed once a week – the whole place was the living embodiment of the old army gag:

'If it moves, salute it; if it doesn't move, pick it up; if you can't pick it up, paint it white.'

On one early morning parade an RSM who was not fond of me, and whose feelings I entirely reciprocated, stopped in front of me, glared at my belt and purred:

'Would you call those brasses clean, lad?'

'I think I'd call them fairly clean, Sir.'

'Fairly clean? *Fairly clean?* Those brasses are FILTHY! You horrible little man, what are you?'

I knew the form, of course – you said 'I'm a horrible little man, Sir,' and then you were let off with a caution. But I didn't feel like calling myself a horrible little man in front of a horrible little man like him, so I stayed silent. His eyes narrowed and he scowled:

'I said you are a horrible little man, what are you?'

No sound from me. He went crimson with fury and shouted:

'Corporal – put this man on a charge. Dumb insolence.'

I got three days 'Extra Parades' which in practice meant cleaning the latrines. It was well worth it. I could handle this silly kind of stuff all right, and the actual signals training was interesting and enjoyable – the bad bit was the boxing.

I had boxed a bit at school, with small success and very little enjoyment. Now I was forced to box again at Catterick with much the same result, except that the enjoyment was even less this time around because when I got hit (which was often) I was being hit by boys a lot bigger and stronger than the boys who had hit me at school. Unfortunately, although I was not very good, I was the only one at my weight who was any good at all, with the result that I found myself one day standing to attention in front of my company commander, Captain Cutter (his name, appropriately enough, is engraved on my brain). He was saying:

'Ah, yes, Quilley. Your physical training instructor tells me you're a useful middle-weight. Our boxing team could do with a useful middle-weight. How would you like to have the honour of representing your regiment against the Green Howards next Saturday?'

'I wouldn't like it at all, Sir.'

'Right, Quilley. You'll be representing your regiment against the Green Howards next Saturday.'

And so I did, of course – and against many other regiments on many other grim Saturdays. I won a few, I lost a few, and then I came up against the amateur middle-weight champion of Sunderland, who broke my nose in the first round. Army boxing is (or was then) only three rounds, but two and a half rounds with a broken nose is, I beg you to believe, very very painful, and I have never, before or since, heard anything so beautiful as the sound of the bell which heralded the end of round three. When I told this story years later to a fellow actor, he said: 'I think you should be paying him ten per cent of your earnings. He did you a favour – he gave you a great nose.'

Catterick Camp actually boasted a theatre among its amenities, and some of the shows, as I remember, were really quite good – certainly better than the ones satirised by us in *Privates on Parade*, or by Windsor Davies' 'Lovely Boys' in *It ain't half hot, Mum*. When my Signals training was finished and I was about to be posted overseas, I stood once more in front of Capt Cutter.

'Wouldn't you like to stay on here, Quilley, and work in the Camp Theatre? Sharpen up your professional skills, eh?'

'No, thank you, Sir,' I replied. 'I think I'd rather go along with my overseas posting – see a bit of the world, you know, Sir?'

I think what I really meant was that I didn't want any more amateur middle-weight champions rearranging my nose.

I was posted to Eritrea, now a province of Ethiopia, but then still an Italian colony. Asmara, the capital, sits on a high plateau not far from the Red Sea, and so enjoys a much more comfortable climate than the sweltering lowlands of the Sudan to the west and the other regions to the north and south. For this reason it housed, at that time, a Rest and Recreation camp for British soldiers on leave who needed to cool off a bit. With its benign weather, combined with all the civilised attractions of an Italian town, including lots of Italian girls, Asmara was regarded with good reason as one of the cushiest billets in Africa. And it was to that very Rest and Recreation camp in Asmara that I was headed.

I never got there.

A bouncy channel crossing to Dieppe, a ravishingly beautiful train journey across France, via Paris, Dijon and Marseilles, and a lazy sea voyage from Toulon to the Nile Delta, ended rather anti-climactically at a Transit Camp in Heliopolis, on the outskirts of Cairo, where I lived pretty miserably for what seemed like a very long time, waiting for the next leg of the journey. As a British Army squaddie in a place like Cairo in 1946 you inevitably saw the sleazy underbelly of Middle Eastern city life, and I knew of course that this had little relevance to the splendours and beauties of the great Egyptian civilisation that had flourished when Britain was a pagan wilderness, but suffice it to say that I was relieved to get away with my boots, my rifle, my kitbag and my paybook all intact and safely in my possession.

At last a beautiful white paddle-steamer straight from Huckleberry Finn wafted us out of the sweaty Cairo suburbs, like a fairy god-mother waving her wand to release Cinderella from her steamy kitchen, and we set off on a magical journey up the Nile – a journey that tourists nowadays pay thousands of pounds to experience. About halfway, just past Aswan, while on watch on the upper deck in the early hours of the morning, I glanced casually to my right, blinked unbelievingly and looked again: I was looking at a group of huge, magnificently carved, seated figures sixty or seventy feet high, hewn directly into the sandstone cliffs which bordered the river. They gazed down in the dawn light placidly, impassively, but with immense authority and power, at our little boat as it paddled bravely upstream.

They were, I discovered later, images of Pharaoh Rameses II, and they had sat in the Temple of Abu Simbel watching the comings and goings of mortals like us along the river since 1250 BC. Ten years after I first saw them the great dam was built at Aswan, and the mighty statues were dug out of the rock and raised two hundred feet up the cliff-face to save them from drowning in the newly-created reservoir. They are safely up there still, but I am quite sure they were happier where they were, part of the living rock beside the ancient waterway where they had lived for three thousand years.

At Wadi Halfa we reached the border – the border between Egypt and the Sudan, between Arab Africa and black Africa, a border which for me had much more than mere geographical significance. I was instantly at home. Smiling black faces helped us from the boat to a Sudan Railways train (made in Birmingham). The same smiling faces served us dinner and showed us how to turn our seats into beds for the night.

At first light next morning I sat on the steps between two carriages, legs dangling rather dangerously over the side, and watched the desert roll by. The railway track was bedded in sand, which meant that the train couldn't go very fast – it never seemed to manage more than about 25mph – so there was ample time to take in the immensity of the breathtaking emptiness which stretched out, apparently for ever, before my astonished English eyes. The cool pink flush of dawn lasted no time at all – the moment the sun cleared the horizon a harsh, invigorating blaze of fire hit the sand like a hammer blow, and the temperature roared up as though a furnace door had opened in my face.

A tiny dot far ahead of us gradually evolved into a man on a camel, plodding steadily northward as we trundled southward. He wore the ubiquitous Sudanese gallabiya and turban, and two huge leather bags hung on each side of his saddle. For perhaps an hour I watched him approach us, pass us, and dwindle to a dot again before disappearing over the northern horizon. Presumably he was heading for Wadi Halfa – perhaps to sell whatever he carried in his saddle-bags – but he seemed to be travelling from nowhere to nowhere, unaware of us, or of anything but his unimaginably distant destination.

We arrived at Khartoum an hour or two after noon, in the hottest part of the day. I had never experienced anything remotely like it – the march from the train, carrying our kitbags to the barrack room on the airfield which was to be our overnight accommodation, was like being grilled on a barbecue. I sat on my bunk under a hopelessly inadequate ceiling fan, thinking, as we all were, that tomorrow, thank God, we would be moving on, and in a day or so would be in Asmara up on that cool plateau, making dates with gorgeous Italian girls.

And yet – and yet – there was something about this place and its people which had already got under my skin. Even on that sweltering march from the train, the feeling I had had on crossing the border – the feeling of being comfortable with these people, of an un-complicated warmth of communication, of mutual affection – had been reinforced. As we marched we had passed simple square houses made of Nile mud and camel dung; women squatted outside cooking over charcoal fires, fanning the flames with palm leaves and waving to us as we passed; tiny naked children marched alongside us, huge dazzling white grins splitting their faces from ear to ear, and when we finally reached the barrack room and sat on our bunks sweating and dreaming of Asmara, a boy burst in carrying a huge, beautiful amphora on his back and crying: 'Limoon! Limoon!' and the lemonade he gave us was made from lemons he had picked that day.

The next morning we were packing our kitbags and preparing to leave for Asmara when a sergeant appeared, wearing on his solar topee a badge depicting a soldier on a camel and the letters SDF – the insignia of the Sudan Defence Force. On his epaulettes was the legend: 'Royal Corps of Signals'. Combined together these slogans declared him to be a sergeant in the Sudan Defence Force Signal Regiment. He greeted us heartily in a ringing tenor voice: 'Right lads – I'm Sgt Bough. The Khartoum Signal Office is short of one W/T operator, and I'm authorised to divert one of you lot into the SDF Signal Regiment. All paybooks onto this table, and the one I pick out is the one who stays here.'

Thirty paybooks went onto the table, Sgt Bough picked one out, and in that resonant tenor which was to be the highspot of countless rowdy evenings over the coming months, he declaimed: '14144244 Signalman Quilley, DC' and my fate was sealed.

The lucky twenty-nine climbed into the truck, waving me goodbye, their cries of 'Sorry, mate' and 'Bad luck, mate' belied by the rapturous smiles of relief and anticipation which wreathed their faces. I collected my gear and walked with Sgt Bough from the airfield to the SDF Barracks, not knowing whether to laugh or cry. I was intensely disappointed, and wildly jealous of the boys on their way up to those airy heights, but at the same time I had a feeling in my bones that staying here just might be more rewarding. I wasn't sure yet. I dumped my kit in the new barrack room, met a few lads and was introduced to Ali, who pronounced himself to be my bearer. He pointed to my sweat-soaked shirt, shorts and socks, and said: 'I take these to dhobi.' 'Dhobi?' 'Laundry – we wash your clothes.' I gave him all the offending garments, and was just about to take a shower when he ran back in, thrusting a bank-note into my hand.

'Ombashi – twenty-five ackers!'

'Er, sorry?'

'Twenty-five piastre note – you left it in your shirt pocket. Very much money!'

He smiled the biggest whitest smile of all the big white smiles I had seen since I came to this country, and I knew then that I was happy to stay.

Believe it or not, there was a theatre in Khartoum, a pleasant little open-air space which went by the grand title of the Khartoum Rep. It was in truth an enthusiastic Amateur Dramatic Society, stoutly supported by my commanding officer, Colonel Ponsonby, and the star actress was (you've already guessed) Mrs Ponsonby, the Colonel's lady. The numbers were made up by some of the young officers and their girlfriends. Other ranks were not encouraged to participate (it was a social club as much as anything, and we didn't quite fit in) but an exception was made in my case, in deference to my impressive history of world-class professional experience, and I was invited to play the young son in John Galsworthy's *Windows*. I don't know whether I was good or bad, but I was certainly a shy and embarrassed fish out of water, and couldn't wait to get back to my mates in the Signal Office.

The Army HQ was right on the banks of the Nile, and the Signal Office occupied a large slice of the ground floor which was regularly visited by water-rats the size of cocker spaniels but not nearly as pretty, who would wander up from the river in the evenings carrying God knows what ghastly tropical diseases, and sit looking hungrily at us with beady little eyes until we hurled the nearest heavy object at their heads, sending them hissing and spitting back to their muddy home in the river bank. When I was promoted to the exalted rank of Acting Unpaid Lance-Corporal I took command of one of the three shifts which manned the Signal Office round the clock, and every third day I was in charge of the night shift, which meant that I spent a lot of time fending off these ugly little brutes; but it also meant that I spent a lot of time in the much more agreeable company of either Anastasia Nasopoulou, Katie Zavridou or Marie Kaprilian, the three delightful young ladies who worked in the Army telephone exchange in the adjoining room. With all the daytime occupants of the building at home in their beds, I was in sole command of the entire HQ, which I suppose gave me a certain cachet. How shall I put it? It was better than boxing, or cleaning latrines.

I learned to sail on the Nile, with the help of Abbas Mohammed el Hassan, one of our motorbike messengers, whose wife presented him with a son not long after I got to know him. As Abbas' boss, I was uniquely privileged to be invited into their house to meet the infant, Ahmed, and over a fiery glass of arrack I became an unofficial uncle. From time to time I would stroll over the bridge to Omdurman and watch the silversmiths making their beautiful filigree jewellery; I would borrow Abbas' bike and roar off into the desert, feeling like Lawrence of Arabia, and watch the sun go down, hoping no sand had got into the petrol tank; during Ramadan I would try to keep the workload as light as possible for the drivers, messengers and telegraphists, who were not allowed to eat or drink during the day and then, when the sun went down, out would come the arrack and the drums, and the singing and dancing would go on all night; I would go to the market and buy dates and lemons, visit a cobbler and have a pair of shoes made on the spot for about half a crown – they died after about six months (I think they were made of cardboard) but they looked lovely while they lasted; I would play the piano in the NAAFI in the evenings, and Ronnie Bough's tenor (he was Ronnie now, not Sgt Bough) would ring out with the Top of the Pops 1947. His favourite was 'September in the Rain':

The leaves of brown
Came tumbling down
Remember?
In September
In the rain.

I could only play in two keys – C (all the white notes) and G flat (all the black ones). I always played 'September in the Rain' in G flat so as to give Ronnie some nice juicy top notes.

Time raced by, suddenly baby Ahmed had grown into a strapping two-year-old, and it was time for me to go home. I found it quite hard to leave. These people were all Mohammedans, happy and relaxed in their religion, but belonging spiritually (it seems to me now) neither to the predominantly Muslim Arab north nor to the predominantly Christian black south. Gentle, honest and tolerant, they have found themselves caught between two warring factions in the terrible conflict which has torn their country apart in recent years. If Ahmed is still alive, he is fifty-five years old. What sort of life does he have in the Sudan of today?

The train this time went, not northward to Wadi Halfa, but eastward to Port Sudan. The same majestically slow progress over the desert sand, the same solitary man on a camel going nowhere (it couldn't really have been the same man, of course, but then again who knows?). Through the Suez Canal, across the Mediterranean, bounce over the Bay of Biscay, round the corner into the Channel, and then – well, it's ridiculous, it's a silly sentimental cliché, but it's like the end of *Madam Butterfly* – you tell yourself you won't be manipulated, you won't cry, but you do; you can't help yourself. The sight of the White Cliffs of Dover after nearly three years away in the desert is just simply too powerful to resist. Vera Lynn rings in your ears, and the tear-ducts refuse to obey the commands of the stiff upper lip.

I spent the whole of the train journey up through Kent to London with my nose pressed against the window and my thirsty eyes drinking in the unbelievable beauty of the green, green fields, green, green trees, apple orchards, sheep, cows, green green England. I hadn't realised how much I loved it.

Chapter 3
Once More into the Breach

THE REVERED, almost mythical figure of Hugh 'Binkie' Beaumont presided elegantly but powerfully over H M Tennent Ltd, the theatre management that dominated the West End in the 1940s and '50s. There were other successful producers of course, most notably Bronson Albery, whose son Donald succeeded him and renamed the New Theatre in St Martin's Lane the Albery after him (or perhaps after himself?) but Binkie was by far the most important impresario in London. He and his partner John Perry were responsible for an impressive string of perceptively chosen and brilliantly presented new plays, as well as handsomely mounted revivals. They always employed the classiest and most talented directors, designers and actors (John Gielgud was their favourite star) and their success rate was formidable. They were the jewel in the crown of the West End theatre.

London in 1949 was a tired old town, still recovering from a long and exhausting war, but for me her allure was irresistible. Try as I might I simply could not settle down again in Ilford with my parents. Only now, as I sit writing this in my big rambling house in Hampstead, with my wife playing the piano in the next room, our granddaughter sleeping upstairs in the room we keep for her whenever she visits us, our son and his wife downstairs awaiting the imminent arrival of their first baby, and our two daughters (both regular visitors) only minutes away, only now do I really understand how lonely and deserted my parents must have felt when I finally gritted my teeth and told them that I needed to move out into a place of my own.

After all, at ten and a bit I had gone away to boarding school, at seventeen I went off to earn my living in Birmingham, at eighteen I disappeared into darkest Africa for three years, and now no sooner was I back in their lives than I was pulling out yet again. My sister (christened Jean but always Paddy to me) had left home years before. It was 1942, halfway through the war, and she was just eighteen. I was home from boarding school for the holidays, and when the doorbell rang it was I who answered it. We had an inkling that she had met someone special, but I was unprepared for the sight of the tall, dashing Army officer who stood on the welcome mat.

'Does a Miss Jean live here?'

'Yes. Yes – Sir!'

(I was deeply impressed by the gold pip on his shoulder – there would be three of them by the end of the Burma campaign.)

'Yes, she does. Sir!'

He was greatly amused, and confessed later that he had half expected me to come to attention and salute. Paddy married Mike Maitland in no time at all and went to live happily in Leigh-on-Sea, much to the dismay and disapproval of our mother, who seemed to believe that the only possible reason for such unseemly haste must be the most unmentionable sin of Having To Get Married. Nothing could have been further from the truth, but she stubbornly refused to come to the wedding, and it was years before she could bring herself to visit Paddy in her new home.

Knowing all this made it even more difficult for me to make the break; I knew that Mum and Dad must be wondering if it had been worth their while bringing a son into the world if they were never going to see him. But finally, after much heart-searching, they understood and wished me well: they saw that I was twenty-one, eager to make my way, and anxious to get closer to the action. And the action, of course, was in the West End.

By some mysterious homing instinct, Stanley Baker and I had found each other again – somewhere in Soho as I remember – and we picked up where we had left off as if we had never been away. We both had some of our Demob money left, so we decided to pool our resources and find a flat that we could share. After endlessly searching the sleazier parts of the capital for something we could afford to rent, we finally landed in up-market South Kensington, though in a distinctly down-market pad – a vast, high-ceilinged barn-like room with a cooker and sink in one corner and a staircase up to a rather spectacular gallery which led to our sleeping space. We decided we would hang a 'Do not disturb' sign at the foot of the stairs whenever one of us might be entertaining a girlfriend. It was scruffy, but it was a great place for big parties, and we had some wonderful ones. One of the more memorable evenings featured a star turn by the Great Shakespearean Busker.

Gallery seats for West End theatres were about 1s/9d or 2s/6d; they were unnumbered – first come, first served – and whoever got in first through the gallery door got into the front row. But if you went to the Box Office early and paid an extra 6d you could hire a little folding stool. You were given a number, then you went and had your tea at Lyons Corner House, and when you came back about an hour before curtain-up you found your little stool set up on the pavement with your number on it, and you sat there at the head of the queue until the gallery doors were opened. So for thirty or forty minutes a sizeable group of theatre-lovers provided an absolutely God-given captive audience for the myriad buskers who enlivened the streets of Soho and the West End: singers; jugglers; Wilson, Keppel and Betty doing sand-dances in Roman togas; and a remarkable man who declaimed the greatest and best-known speeches from Shakespeare in a splendidly stentorian baritone, usually a bit drunk but always word perfect, and with great understanding of the form of the verse and the emotions of the characters. He was always good for 2d or 3d when the hat came round at the end of his turn.

Stanley and I invited him to one of our soirées, and he was a big hit. Up on our gallery, a wonderfully dominant platform for a natural orator and show-off, he went through *Hamlet*, *Lear* and *Macbeth*, and then launched into Mark Antony's great speech from *Julius Caesar*:

> Friends, Romans, countrymen, lend me your ears:
> I come to bury Caesar, not to praise him.
> The evil that men do lives after them –
> The good is oft interred with their bones –

at which point fatigue, emotion and whisky overtook him, and he somersaulted gracefully down the entire length of the staircase, landed on the floor, and rose triumphantly to his feet crying: 'So let it be with Caesar!' to receive a well-deserved standing ovation.

But our flat was not just an ace party venue, it was the engine-room of our campaign to get ourselves back into the theatre business after all those years away. Between us we must have written to every single repertory theatre in the country, and not one of them wanted to know us. By contrast, our old friend Paul Scofield was now an established star. Just after we left Birmingham for our Army service, Barry Jackson had been asked to take on the Shakespeare Festival Theatre at Stratford-upon-Avon, and very wisely he took Paul Scofield and Peter Brook along with him. They both had enormous success there, and as a result Peter was at the beginning of a magnificent national and international career, and Paul was a fully-fledged West

End leading man, currently playing Alexander the Great in Terence Rattigan's play *Adventure Story*.

Stanley somehow wangled himself a job in that production as a walk-on (literally carrying a spear) and it became clear that I, too, would have to start bringing some money into our ménage if our glittering reputation for lavish entertaining was to be maintained. So I wrote to H M Tennent asking for an audition. They operated an admirable system whereby, every six months or so, they sent a postcard to everyone who had written in and invited them all to a mass audition, girls one day, boys on another. I duly received my postcard and turned up at the Globe Theatre (now the Gielgud) in Shaftesbury Avenue on the morning of the appointed day, together with about a hundred hopeful young men who were all much more confident, experienced and charismatic than I. My chances were zero.

The morning wore on, and one boy after another was ushered onto the stage from the wings, introduced and ticked off on the Stage Manager's list. Each one would launch eagerly into his chosen set piece, and after a couple of minutes a voice from the stalls would interrupt and say: 'Thank you dear – we'll let you know.' The voice belonged to Daphne Rye, the Casting Director, the Keeper of the gates of Paradise, the Bouncer at the door of the nightclub, the Great Examiner whose nod of approval was the passport to West End fame, and whose thumbs down meant a life of cheap digs and provincial Rep.

Halfway through the morning the boy ahead of me in the queue, who was terribly nervous and had been silently mouthing his lines for the last hour and a half, was called on and introduced.

'What are you going to do for me, dear?'

'Um, *Henry the Fifth* all right, Miss Rye?'

'Yes, all right, dear – off you go.'

'Once more into the... um... um...'

'Never mind, dear – start again.'

'Thank you, Miss Rye. Once more into the *breach*, dear friends, once more, or close the... um... close the *wall* up with our English... um... um...'

This went on for an agonising two or three minutes, during which he dried about fifteen times, until blessed relief came:

'Thank you, dear – that gives me a very good idea what you can do. We'll let you know.'

'I'm very sorry, Miss Rye – I only got the postcard this morning.'

I was sweating for the poor wretched boy, who was close to tears as he came off into the wings, but there was no time for commiserations – I was next. The Stage Manager led me on and announced me:

'Mr Denis Quigley.'

'Er, no – Quilley.'

'Mm?'

'My name's Quilley – double L–E–Y.'

'Ah, sorry – Mr Denis *Quilley.*'

'Right,' said The Voice. 'I'm *really* glad we've got that sorted out. Now what you are you going to do for me, dear?'

'Would *Hamlet* be all right, Miss Rye?'

'Ye-e-ss, all right, dear,' she sighed, in a tone of voice which only just managed to conceal her true feelings, which obviously were: 'Oh God, the morning's only half over and I've had fifteen bloody Hamlets already. Not another one, *please*!'

We were not off to a good start. Never mind, Hamlet was a trusty old friend. I had been beautifully introduced to him in my schooldays by Don Francombe and John Gielgud, and I now understood him rather better, having lived a little in the interim:

> Oh what a rogue and peasant slave am I!
> Is it not monstrous that this player here,
> But in a fiction, in a dream of passion,
> Could force his soul so to his own conceit
> That from her working all his visage wan'd...

I got about half way through, and was just coming up to the juicy bit: 'Bloody, bawdy villain, Remorseless, lecherous, treacherous, kindless villain. Oh vengeance!' where I would really let rip and show how I could tear a passion to tatters, when the inevitable happened:

'Thank you, dear, that gives me a very good idea what you can do.'

My shoulders slumped, I headed disconsolately towards the exit, and she added, almost as an afterthought:

'Come and see me in my office at half past two this afternoon.'

I stopped in my tracks, poleaxed, and managed to stammer: 'Half past two – yes, right, thank you – half past two,' and stumbled into the wings, where I was met by fifty pairs of murderously envious eyes.

At half past two on the dot a rickety little lift juddered its way from the foyer of the Globe up to an unsuspected little eyrie under the roof which looked down over a panoramic view of Shaftesbury Avenue. What perfect symbolism, I thought dizzily: theatreland was at my feet. Daphne Rye turned out to be a charming middle-aged lady whose motherly exterior belied a very astute brain and an encyclopaedic knowledge of the theatre business. She shook my hand, sat me down, and hit me straight between the eyes with her opening line:

'How would you like to work with Mr Gielgud, dear?'

Well, what a silly question. No answer was required, really. None was forthcoming, anyway – I was struck dumb. I raised my eyebrows and nodded sagely in what I hoped was a non-committal manner, implying, 'Tell me more and I'll see if my manager thinks its worth my while,' and she continued:

'We're doing a new play called *The Lady's not for Burning* by a marvellous writer called Christopher Fry. Mr Gielgud is going to direct it and play the leading role, and for the juvenile lead we've got a very good new boy called Richard Burton. We need someone to understudy him – would you like to do it?'

High-level talks followed for all of five minutes, and the sum of eight pounds a week which I finally forced out of her by shrewd and ruthless negotiation seemed acceptable to both sides. After all, a hundred per cent increase from my first job to my second (even with three years in between) was quite impressive. I walked down the Avenue to Piccadilly Circus underground bursting with pride and joy. My foot was on the first rung of the ladder.

When I reached the wings on my first day of rehearsal my head swam. John Gielgud, Pamela Brown, Nora Nicholson, Claire Bloom, Richard Burton, Eliot Makeham, Peter Bull, Harcourt Williams (who used to run The Old Vic in the '30s) and Esmé Percy (who earlier still had been in the original productions of some of Bernard Shaw's greatest plays) – all these eminent people were standing on the stage chatting wittily in their elegant clothes, completely at ease with each other, having already been in rehearsal for a week before I arrived, and totally unaware of the clumsy, shy boy in his Demob suit standing in the wings, shuffling his feet and trying to summon up the courage to step on stage and introduce himself.

Divine intervention was at hand, in the shape of a lovely girl who walked over to me, smiled a ravishing smile and said:

'Hallo – can I have your telephone number?'

'Oh, *yes!*' I grinned lasciviously.

'No, no,' she laughed. 'My name is Stella Chapman, and I'm understudying Pamela Brown and Claire Bloom, but I'm also the Assistant Stage Manager and I need your address and phone number for the records.'

Ah, well. I gave her my phone number, and six months later we got married. Mum said:

'It won't last, Den. You're a boy who likes his freedom – I give it two years.'

It's still going strong fifty years later, Mum.

We got married on a Saturday morning. Stella had a throat infection and was not in good shape, so her father, who was giving her away, administered emergency medication. As I waited in the front row of the stalls in St Paul's Church, Onslow Square, listening to the organ playing the 'Wedding March,' I became aware of a heady aroma of brandy wafting up the aisle towards me. Stella greeted me with a happy, happy smile, we went through the service without missing a trick, and after a convivial wedding breakfast we staggered to the Globe Theatre just in time for the Saturday matinée. Ah – the glamour of Showbiz.

The Lady's not for Burning created quite a stir. The war had been over for more than three years, but food and clothes were still rationed, 'utility' furniture was still in the shops, dried eggs and Spam were exotic treats, rumours of a delivery of bananas caused instant queues round the block, and girls were running up dresses from off-the-ration RAF parachute silk.

Everything was very prosaic and grey, and then suddenly Christopher Fry ravished our ears and our hearts with language: beautiful, witty, touching, poetic language of a kind that we thought had disappeared from the English theatre.

THOMAS: Out here is a sky so gentle
    Five stars are ventured on it. I can see
    The sky's pale belly glowing and growing big,
    Soon to deliver the moon. And I can see
    A glittering smear, the snail-trail of the sun
    Where it crawled with its golden shell into the hills.
    A darkening land sunken into prayer
    Lucidly in dewdrops of one syllable,
    Nunc dimittis. I see twilight, madam.

JENNET: What can we see in this light?
    Nothing, I think, except flakes of drifting fear,
    The promise of oblivion.

THOMAS: Nothing can be seen
    In the thistledown, but the rough-head thistle comes
    Rest in that riddle. I can pass to you
    Generations of roses in this wrinkled berry.
    There: now you hold in your hand a race
    Of summer gardens, it lies under centuries
    Of petals. What is not, you have in your palm.

I suppose I view this particular play through rose-coloured spectacles, for obvious reasons, but half a century later it still seems to me to be very beautiful. At the time some of us thought it might be the spearhead of a revival of poetic drama; that never happened, of course, indeed it was only a few years later that *Look Back in Anger* caused a seismic shift in a completely opposite (and in its own way equally exciting) direction.

But *The Lady* had a long and successful run – long enough for Stella and me to move into the roles of the young lovers when Richard Burton and Claire Bloom went on to bigger things. By then we had been understudying for about nine months, but John Gielgud rehearsed us very thoroughly for our take-over.

'How is it coming, Mr Gielgud?' I asked him nervously after a day or so.

'It's very nice, Squilley.' (He called me Squilley, for reasons I never dared to question.) 'It's very nice and Norman and rounded – if we can get it just a little bit more Gothic and pointed, I think we'll be there.'

The great Esmé Percy had just one scene at the end of the play as a hilariously drunken rag-and-bone man. My job was to push him on in a wheelbarrow, tip him out onto his feet and let him get on with the scene. Poor Esmé had just lost his mother, and was very unhappy and drinking rather heavily to drown his sorrows. On one particular evening his sorrows were well and truly drowned, and he was in no mood to climb into my wheelbarrow.

'Please, Mr Percy,' I implored him as our cue got closer, 'please get into the wheelbarrow.' He waved me away imperiously, mouthing dark and unfathomable imprecations.

'*Please*, Mr Percy.' More muttered refusals. Finally, as our entrance line inexorably arrived, I took a deep breath, picked him up bodily and dumped him into the barrow – fortunately I was young and strong and he was a very small man. I wheeled him on, tipped the barrow up very carefully with one hand while holding on to him with the other to make sure he stayed on his feet, and stood back to watch with my fingers crossed.

He launched into the scene with brio, achieving a very fair approximation to Mr Fry's script, and all went swimmingly and quite enjoyably until, carried away on a wave of euphoria at a climactic moment, he produced an arm-waving gesture of such wild extravagance that his little body rotated like a spinning-top and his glass eye flew out. It shot out of its socket like a cannonball straight towards the audience, bounced gaily three or four times and came to rest with a resounding clunk in the trough of the footlights.

The scene stopped dead; nobody spoke or moved, and the entire audience held its breath in disbelief. Time stood still for a while, and then I decided that, as the character I was playing was at the bottom of the pecking order in the household, I was the one who ought to do something, so I set off downstage towards the footlights to retrieve the missing eye. This instantly galvanised Esmé back into action, and he flung me aside with a roar and went for it himself. He got down on his hands and knees, rummaged around for a while, finally found the eye, and then couldn't get up: as well as being a little under the weather, he had a gammy leg which even at the best of times would have made the manoeuvre a severe test. I trotted back down to the footlights and helped him to his feet; he hurled me away even more wildly than before, polished the eye on his shirt-sleeve, popped it back in, finished the scene with stunning bravura and made his exit to a storm of applause.

The stage manager persuaded him to wear a rather dashing eye-patch for the rest of the run.

When that run came to an end I turned down the offer of another understudy job. I had tasted blood – I had heard the laughter and applause of a West End audience, and I didn't want to get filed in H M Tennent's 'Useful Understudy' pigeonhole. I wanted to go out and prove myself. 'Just thought you might like a job, dear,' said a slightly miffed Daphne Rye, and as things turned out, she had a point: starring roles were not immediately on offer.

Stella, who is a whirlwind shorthand typist, went out temping, and I sold toys at Selfridges for a while before graduating to the less exciting but marginally more lucrative profession of washing-up. I cycled every morning from our newly acquired bedsitter in Maida Vale (27s/6d week, shared bathroom) to Park Lane, where I plied my trade in one of the most glamorous and expensive hotels in the world. On each floor there was a pantry to which room service meals travelled up from the basement kitchens by dumb waiter, to be prettied up by the far-from-dumb floor waiters with napkins, cutlery and flowers, and wheeled along to the punters.

I arrived each morning at 8am and set to work at my two huge, square, rather handsome sinks made of beautiful dark wood – teak at a guess. I washed up the breakfasts, had a short break and then dealt with the lunches, finishing by mopping the floor at about 4pm. On my first day I made the serious mistake of taking my lunch-break in the staff canteen, down in the bowels of the earth next to the kitchens. Never in my life, anywhere – at boarding school, in Boy Scout camps, in the Army, in Egyptian greasy spoons, in theatre digs, in motorway service stations – never have I tasted such disgusting food as the workers in that hotel were expected to eat while supplying the customers upstairs with some of the fanciest meals in London.

From that day on I breakfasted on cornflakes from the pantry cupboard, and lunched on the succulent leftovers that came back from the bedrooms. I washed up James Mason's lunch one day; when we were filming Agatha Christie's *Evil under the Sun* together in Mallorca about thirty years later, I told him of this great moment in my young life, and he said in that suave, velvety voice of his: 'Oh, my dear boy, if only I'd known I would have come and given you a hand.'

That really would have given the waiters and the cleaning lady something to talk about.

The waiters were hard-working and amusing, and quite enjoyed bossing an out-of-work actor about; occasionally they would even ask me to 'give us a bit of Shakespeare, then' and when I did they would greet it with loud, ironic but friendly applause; the sweet, motherly cleaning lady was always on my side, saying: 'Don't take the piss out of 'im – 'e's a nice boy.' One way and another, time passed very pleasantly in our little pantry.

On about my third or fourth day a cheerful young chap turned up carrying a metal cylinder on his back with a tube and nozzle attached.

'Mornin' mate – stand back.' I stood back, as commanded, and he sprayed an evil-smelling blue cloud all over the sinks and the surrounding wall. When he had finished I started back towards my waiting dishes, saying, 'Is that it?'

'Nah, nah, keep back mate, keep well back.' I kept well back, and a few moments later a million cockroaches crawled out from behind my beautiful sinks, rolled over on the floor and died. The lad produced a sack from a capacious pocket, swept the sad little corpses into it, and waved goodbye, saying, 'See yer nex' week.' And so he did, next week and every week, working his way from the top floor to the bottom, ending up, presumably, in the basement kitchens, where I suspect a few of his little victims ended up in the cooking pots of the staff canteen.

The food at the trattoria in the Piazza della Signoria in Florence was in a rather different league: grilled prawns were the perfect prelude to a dish of spaghetti al sugo washed down with chianti ruffino, and veal scallopini alla Marsala led naturally to zabaglione and a double espresso with a glass of grappa. Boys and girls rode dashingly past the outdoor tables on their Vespa scooters – the newest and sexiest way of getting around town – and the view across the square was of the Palazzo Vecchio, its colonnade filled with masterpieces of sculpture by Michelangelo and Della Robbia.

I was here to play Fabian, the smallest and most boring part in Shakespeare's *Twelfth Night*, at Florence's Teatro Pergola. While chewing on a delicious leftover chicken leg in my cosy pantry in Park Lane I had read an item in *The Stage* newspaper telling me that the Old Vic company was sending a tour of *Twelfth Night* to Florence, Milan, Turin, Venice, Rome and Trieste. This looked like a good gig, and somehow or other (I forget how) I managed to get myself into it.

Celia Johnson was a beautiful wide-eyed Viola, Roger Livesey a fruity gravel-voiced Toby Belch, Robert Eddison a funny and touching Aguecheek, and the legendary Ernest Milton (in what I think may have been his last performance) was a Malvolio from another era – a Malvolio who would have been admired by Irving and Forbes-Robertson. He was also, I must say, much admired by me and by the opening night audience, who found 'La Dodicessima Notte' greatly to their liking, despite the fact that about half way through the evening the lighting cues got out of synch, so that every time Ernest came on for a soliloquy there was a blackout, and every scene-change took place in a blaze of light. This continued for about a quarter of an hour, while the only member of our company who spoke serviceable Italian frantically tried to explain the situation to the poor beleaguered lighting men. All was well in the end, and the applause at curtain-fall was ecstatic.

The British Council had laid on an official reception after the opening, with lots of local dignitaries, so by the time we got out of the theatre it was about one in the morning. A few of us (the younger, non-starry half of the cast-list) wandered off in search of a glass of wine. The first café we came to was just closing; the tables were all being cleared, and a four-piece band were packing their instruments away and looking forward to going home after a hard night's work. When I asked the waiter in my halting Italian whether we were in time to get a drink, he smiled 'Si, si – certamente!,' threw a cloth over a table and fetched a couple of bottles and half a dozen glasses. As he did so, the band looked at each other, nodded, unpacked their instruments and played for us for half an hour.

I think it was in that moment that my love of Italy and all things Italian was born. The easy, natural generosity of spirit, the uncomplicated enjoyment of the good things of life – food, wine, music, friendship, children – warms the heart and comforts the soul. How pale and drab our lives would have been without Verdi, Puccini, Piero della Francesca, Botticelli, Michelangelo, Fellini, Pasolini, Pavarotti – even the names, to an Anglo-Saxon ear, are exotically beautiful.

In Venice we played in the exquisite little La Fenice opera house. When Charlie Phipps, our head carpenter in charge of the stage crew, was asked by his mates back in London how he had enjoyed Venice, he replied: 'Bloody awful get-in. All the bloody scenery has to go in by bloody water! Pretty place, though, and very nice people.'

A few years later I was able to share the delights of Italy with Stella. We sat up most of the night travelling third-class in the train, arriving in Florence in the early hours of the morning. We had picked a pensione with a pin from the price range we could afford – the Pensione Isola. We stood in the dark, deserted street outside a huge, imposing stone Renaissance façade with elaborate wrought-iron grilles over the windows, and an enormous oak door. I tugged at the bell-pull beside the door, and a melodious peal echoed through the dark and silent rooms beyond. After a long pause a light glowed through one of the windows, bolts were drawn and the great door swung open, revealing a small elderly gentleman with immaculate white hair wearing an immaculate white jacket.

'Signor e Signora Quilley? Benvenuti – Avanti, avanti.'

We walked into a high-ceilinged, wood-panelled hallway where an equally immaculate little white-haired lady greeted us.

'Buona sera. Io sono Isola Focardi.'

Her name was Isola – the pensione was named after her. 'Ecco la chiave.' She gave us our key, and we climbed upstairs to a cosy little room and fell instantly asleep.

I awoke to the sound of women singing. Fascinated, I tiptoed to the window and opened the shutters, and my eyes and ears were assailed by dazzling beauty. I felt like Kirk Douglas in that marvellous scene from *Lust for Life* when Van Gogh, after travelling from Holland and arriving after dark in the South of France, opened his shutters the next morning and saw for the first time the olive groves, the pine trees and the golden light of Provence. I whispered Stella over to the window, and we stood on the tiny balcony like children staying up late to watch a grown-up party.

We were looking over the garden of a convent, and the nuns were walking round the garden singing their morning prayers; the early morning sun gently touched the convent walls with pale pink light while the rest of the city slept. Later in the day we climbed up to the Piazzale Michelangelo, where you can stand beside the statue of David (the original lives in state in the gallery of the Accademia) and look across the whole panorama of this miraculously beautiful and civilised city, with Brunelleschi's dome and Giotto's bell tower sitting majestically in pride of place at its centre, and wonder how we lost the art of building into the landscape and enhancing it instead of ruining it.

Italy loved Stella. In villages, boys would ride by on their Vespas, catch sight of her and ride by again, no hands, just to impress her.

On the beach at Taormina in Sicily, fishermen plied her with songs and offers of night fishing trips. In Sardinia she was known to all the hotel staff not as Signora Quilley, but as *La Mignona* – the sweet one.

I began to get the feeling I had married the right girl.

Chapter 4
Slings and Arrows

TODAY, THE YOUNG VIC is the name of a rough, but sweet and friendly little theatre-in-the-round just along the road from the Old Vic in The Cut, a bustling and energetic street a stone's throw from Waterloo Station. But in the early '50s, before that little theatre was built, The Young Vic was the name of a company of actors.

The war-damaged Old Vic had been roughly repaired, and the resident acting company was run by not one, not two, but three eminent directors – George Devine, Michel St Denis and Glen Byam Shaw. It was under their aegis that I had toured Italy in *Twelfth Night*, and when that tour ended they offered me a choice: I could stay with the Old Vic company playing bits and pieces, or I could join the Young Vic and play leading roles. The Young Vic was a touring company in provincial theatres and occasionally in local schools, and its actors were, as the name suggested, younger members of the organisation who were happy to tour in return for playing more rewarding roles than they would be offered in the parent company.

Naturally, I opted for the Young Vic, and found myself playing the juvenile lead in an exuberant dramatisation of Robert Louis Stevenson's novel *The Black Arrow*, and Gratiano in *The Merchant of Venice*. Playing Bassanio in the *The Merchant* was Keith Michell, who many years later was a definitive Henry the Eighth on television, and Shylock's daughter Jessica was a radiantly beautiful young June Brown, now the nation's best-loved cockney chain-smoker, Dot in *EastEnders*.

If you are ever asked to perform *The Merchant of Venice* in a school hall at 10 in the morning to an audience of a hundred eight-to-ten year olds, resist the temptation, even if they offer you a free lunch. The name of the town and the school are mercifully expunged from my memory, but what I do recall with blinding clarity is that Lorenzo entered with Jessica and said:

> How sweet the moonlight sleeps upon this bank!
> Here will we sit, and let the sound of music
> Creep in our ears.

As he sat, and gracefully extended his hand for Jessica to recline beside him, all Hell broke loose.

'Go on – give 'er one!' they shouted. 'Get your leg over!' and other unprintable exhortations. The ensuing speeches, containing some of Shakespeare's most dazzling poetry and wisest human insights, passed unheard, drowned by the cries of these alarmingly knowledgeable and lascivious children.

As I waited in the wings for my entrance I became aware of a spattering sound on the stage. Was a lamp sparking? Was rain coming through the roof? No, pea-shooters were being deployed (this was 1951 when such innocuous toys still existed). The missiles landed with impressive accuracy all over and around the moonlit bank until Lorenzo and Jessica, who had long since given up trying to play the scene, finally rose from their grassy bower and tiptoed off hand in hand through the carpet of peas into the wings, and the cacophony subsided enough for the rest of us to get the play back on course.

The Black Arrow faced a rather different but equally tough test in front of an audience of very spritely university undergraduates at the Arts Theatre in Cambridge. It fell to me to bring the first act to a close by nobly declaiming to Keith Michell: 'Never fear – I will deliver your message, and I will guard it with my life!' Then, in my romantic period cloak and hat, with trusty sword at my side, I made a dashing exit through the door upstage centre, turned in the doorway and waved, crying, 'Farewell, Will, farewell!' and ran offstage. (Cue for fall of curtain, storms of applause, interval of 15 minutes.)

At this particular performance in Cambridge the first act had been going really well, and I was determined to make that exit more dramatic than it had ever been, and show these young intellectuals what the excitement of live theatre was all about. I delivered the line with great panache, turned and ran upstage, missed the door completely and cannoned straight into the back wall which, being constructed of painted canvas on a wooden frame, floated slowly and gracefully to the floor, revealing two startled stagehands in their shirtsleeves, each carrying a counterweight in one hand and a brace in the other, preparing to dismantle the wall and change the set for Act II. Needless to say, for the undergrads this was the high point of the academic year. They went off to their interval pints of bitter whooping with delight, and when I made my re-entrance at the beginning of the second act they gave me a standing ovation. Little did they know that even more exquisite delights were in store.

Not for nothing was this show called *The Black Arrow*: arrows were everywhere. If you were lucky enough to be one of those who got shot during this action-packed evening you had the most marvellous death scene. An arrow was strapped to your side with a spring-loaded hinge at the top end, on your chest, and a clip holding the feathered end down on your thigh. When the audience's eyes were all on your antagonist on the other side of the stage drawing his bow as though preparing to unleash an arrow, you pulled a ring to release *your* arrow, which instantly sprang up into a horizontal position, went 'Boingg,' and stuck quivering in your chest. Now that all eyes were on you, your assassin could unobtrusively hide his arrow up his sleeve, and all you had to do was cry 'Aargh!' and fall to the floor to receive a really rather easily-won round of applause.

Since I was playing the indestructible young hero, this cheap but enjoyable little treat was denied me; however I did have the privilege of taking part in a Great Arrow Moment in the second act, barely half an hour after my sensational demolition of the upstage wall. The best trick arrow in the whole show was one which appeared to be shot in through a window from outside and landed, not in someone's chest, but in the middle of a table around which four of us were sitting. This dazzling illusion was most ingeniously contrived: there was a crash of breaking glass, produced by a stage manager smashing a beer bottle with a hammer in the wings, a broken pane was slid into the window, and when all four of us looked up at the broken window, that same stage manager pulled a wire which ran along the floor and up the table leg, releasing a flap which covered a little trough in the table top concealing (yes!) a spring-loaded arrow which then sprang up, went 'Boingg' and quivered vertically in the middle of the table, with a message attached to it which one of us had to remove and read.

Just in case this brilliant device didn't work, a spare arrow, complete with message, was concealed under the table. It was absolutely inevitable, of course, that the one and only occasion on which this rather inexperienced understudy arrow would ever be called upon to perform was in the presence of this merry group of irreverent and boisterous young students. We heard the glass break. We all looked up and saw the broken window-pane. We all looked down at the table and saw – nothing. (Small laugh from the audience.) Then (unwisely, but we were a little stressed) the four of us looked frantically off into the wings in unison, as if to say 'Where's our arrow?' (laugh number two, rather bigger). We saw the stage manager tugging manfully but unsuccessfully on his wire and mouthing: 'Use the spare – use the spare!' The actor who had to read the message reached under the table, grabbed the spare, and with an elaborate but unconvincing mime pretended to pull it up out of the table-top (laugh number three – well, more of a groan really). He then detached the message and began to read it aloud, and as he read it the flap on the table gently and shyly crept open, and the recalcitrant arrow began a very, very slow journey from the horizontal to the vertical, in a series of tired little creaks, accompanied all the way by cheers and the longest slow handclap I have ever heard, even in my wildest dreams.

If any members of that Cambridge audience are still alive, and should happen by any chance to be reading this, I will gladly refund them the price of their tickets, adjusted for inflation.

I declined the offer of another season with the Young Vic: I had only been married for a couple of years, and had done enough touring for the time being. But there was also another reason why I felt a change of direction was needed – I wanted to find out whether there might be a rewarding career for me in the musical theatre. I had inherited from my parents a natural singing voice and a good musical ear, and it had always seemed a shame not to put these modest gifts to some use. Consequently, when I got back to London I went up for every musical audition I could find. Stella was often trying for the same show, and sometimes we would audition together – we sang well with each other, and we were less nervous singing a duet than going solo. If nothing else, it was unusual enough to help the producers to remember us. ('Ah yes – the young couple who sang a duet together. Yes, charming – sorry, nothing for you in this show.')

We once duetted for the great Ivor Novello, then at the height of his fame as the composer of *The Dancing Years*, *Perchance to Dream* and *King's Rhapsody*, in which he was currently playing the lead. He was wildly enthusiastic and bounded up on to the stage to congratulate us: we were both to be in his new show, he declared; he was writing it now and it would begin rehearsals in a few months' time, when he looked forward to meeting us again. Alas – a few weeks later he died, the new show unwritten. His dresser took the message he used to hang on the dressing-room door when he was resting between shows on matinée days, and posted it on the company notice-board for all to see. It read: 'Quiet please; the master is sleeping.'

Eventually we had the great good fortune to audition for Wendy Toye – dancer, choreographer, theatre director, opera director, film director and one of the great ladies of the English theatre, worthy to be mentioned in the same breath with Lilian Baylis and Ninette de Valois. Wendy was casting a light-hearted musical romp about Samuel Pepys called *And So To Bed*, starring the great gravel-voiced comedian Leslie Henson, and the immediate outcome of our joint audition was that Stella landed a very nice supporting role as Lady Castlemaine's maid, and I got into the chorus, with a one-line walk-on part as an ancient retainer with bad feet who got one laugh (on a good night). But Wendy's influence in the long term was absolutely crucial. On discovering that I had never taken singing lessons she advised me – nay, commanded me – to start doing so at once. If I acquired a proper technique to support my pleasant but untrained voice through the rigours of singing a big part in a big theatre eight times a week, she was convinced that I would land leading roles in West End musicals. I was still in my early twenties, and there was plenty of time to learn, so I took her at her word, and began looking for a teacher.

The relationship between a singing teacher and his pupil is a very delicate and personal one. An instrumentalist's ideas and emotions are conveyed to his audience through an intermediary – an ivory key activating a felt-tipped hammer; a bow of horse-hair drawn across strings of metal or gut; a column of air vibrating in a tube of wood or brass – but the singer has no such intermediary: he himself is the instrument. Air sucked into the lungs is pushed up the windpipe by the diaphragm, passes through two delicate little strips of cartilage in the throat, and continues upwards to resonate in the nasal and frontal sinuses in the head.

This crucial difference is so obvious that it might seem hardly worth mentioning, but the enormous implications of that difference are perhaps less obvious. Take the elementary act of changing the pitch of a note. The pianist achieves this by moving his finger from one key, which he knows produces a note of a certain pitch, to another key higher up the keyboard which produces a note of a higher pitch. The violinist achieves it by putting a finger higher up the string, or by crossing to another string which is tuned higher, and the wind player presses a different combination of keys or valves. But the singer changes pitch simply by taking thought. If he says to himself 'I'm going to sing a note an octave higher than the one I'm singing now,' he simply does so, and by some mysterious and magical process (the physics of which, I need hardly tell you, I cannot begin to fathom) those two little strips of cartilage in his throat which we call the vocal cords instantly vibrate at precisely double the frequency, and out comes the note an octave higher. With very, very few exceptions the singer has no idea how this comes about – he is certainly not aware of giving his vocal cords instructions to vibrate at a different speed. He thinks it, he wills it, and it happens.

In the same way any change of emotion, from joy to sadness, from despair to triumph, from love to hate, if truly felt by the singer, instantly and inevitably changes the colour, the timbre, the volume of the voice – and again it happens simply by taking thought. To be sure, it takes years to learn how to sing *properly* – to use the muscles of the diaphragm and the rib-cage, to keep the throat open and relaxed, to place the voice unerringly in the resonating chambers so as to be able to sing for long periods without strain – but in fact virtually everyone can sing after a fashion with no training whatsoever, and men have done so since the dawn of time. Seen in this light, singing seems to be music-making at its most primitive and unsophisticated, but it is also music-making at its most personal and spontaneous, and when the unique extra ingredient of language is added to the mix, it becomes music-making at its most subtle and powerful. From the sublime simplicity of 'My love is like a red, red rose' to the heroic grandeur of the 'Hallelujah Chorus,' this is music which speaks from heart to heart direct, without let or hindrance. Whether it be Jussi Björling singing Puccini, or a group of Welsh miners singing 'Men of Harlech,' or my father singing 'Abide with Me' as he mended my shoes, it is surely the purest and simplest expression of feeling we are capable of.

Not surprisingly, then, if teacher and pupil are not of the same way of thinking – mentally, emotionally and musically – the working relationship cannot be fruitful. Of course a purely mechanical technique can be taught by anyone to anyone, but we are talking here not just of 'How?' but of 'Why?' and of choices.

Do you want to stress the meaning of this phrase rather than that one? If so, why? Does the overall meaning of the poet's words, or the composer's response to those words, warrant it? Would a sudden pianissimo here, rather than a gradual diminuendo, be justified, or are you just trying to create an effect for its own sake? These are the sort of questions which only two like-minded people can properly answer. Luckily, I found Ernst Urbach.

Ernst was a cultured, charming Viennese Jewish gentleman whose family had come to England in the '30s. He was interred during the War under Regulation 18B as an 'enemy alien' but survived with his digestion ruined and his love of England miraculously undiminished. He was steeped in the Austro-German musical tradition, and after a tough period of learning about breathing, abdominal support, nasal resonance and all the rest of it, we happily began to explore the riches of Brahms, Duparc and Fauré, Schumann's *Dichterliebe*, Schubert's *Schöne Müllerin* and Hugo Wolf's *Spanisches Liederbuch*. For me it was an ecstatic voyage of discovery, for Ernst a revisiting of old friends he had been intimate with for as long as he could remember. We once sat listening to a recording of the great tenor, Beniamino Gigli, and I said, 'Oh God, Ernst, I'd give an arm and a leg for a tenor voice like that.' (I am, of course, a standard-issue baritone.) 'With some things I can help you, my dear,' he replied, 'but for this you must apply to a higher authority.'

Quite apart from the excellent lessons and the congenial company, a major advantage of being one of Ernst's pupils was that he had access to the semi-public dress rehearsals of all the operas at Covent Garden and Sadler's Wells (then the home of the English National Opera, now based in the Coliseum). These rehearsals were always full: the audiences were made up of 'Friends of Covent Garden' (or of Sadler's Wells), students and professors from all the major music colleges, visiting musicians and singers from overseas, the theatre management and front of house staff, and a few freeloaders like me. It was in every respect just like an actual performance (full costume and make-up, full stage scenery and lighting, full orchestra) with the one delightful difference that it was free. There were occasional hiccups and mix-ups of course, but that only made it more fascinating and exciting – one was after all watching work in progress rather than the finished article, and the workers were some of the greatest artists in the world.

Two of these splendid experiences have stayed indelibly in my mind after all these years – Wagner was the composer on both occasions. *The Valkyrie* at Covent Garden was a magnificent international affair: Wotan, the King of the Gods, was sung by the great German bass-baritone Hans Hotter, a tall commanding figure and a fine authoritative actor with massive stage presence and a glorious voice to match. Truly an awe-inspiring King of the Gods. His daughter Brunnhilde, the leader of the Valkyries, was played by Margaret Harshaw, a distinguished American soprano. She was a big lady with a big voice, and this being a straightforward production with no modernistic gimmicks, she was dressed in the traditional manner – a full-length military-looking robe, two massive circular breast-plates protecting her impressive chest, and a pudding-basin helmet with two fearsome horns sprouting from the sides. To complete the picture of the indomitable warrior-queen she carried a spear about eight feet long.

We were into Act II and the famous 'Abschied,' Wotan's farewell to his beloved but rebellious daughter. The Act II set was a rocky terrain with a lot of ups and downs to be negotiated, and Miss Harshaw (who had probably had grossly inadequate rehearsal, as is too often the case even now with international opera productions) was having some trouble finding her way around. She tried using her spear as a kind of alpenstock but it was so enormous that it proved to be a liability rather than a mountaineering aid. 'Lebewohl, meine Tochter' (Farewell, my daughter) sang Hotter, with ravishing tone and beautifully controlled emotion, and back came the reply from his daughter in a voice straight from the vibrant streets of New York City: 'What the hell am I supposed to do with this goddamn spear?'

This poignant plea seemed to be addressed not to Hotter, nor to the conductor, but to the world in general, and certainly we in the audience empathised with her – what indeed was she supposed to do with the goddamn spear? Had I been in her place I think I might well have been asking the same question. The conductor was still valiantly urging on his players in the orchestra pit, who of course were missing, as they always do, the wonderful drama going on just above their heads. Without breaking the rhythm of his beat he managed to say: 'Could you keep going please Miss Harshaw – we're trying to time this act.' 'Okay, OKAY! I'll keep GOING!' replied the diva and turned her attention back to the drama. Hotter had continued singing and acting with magisterial indifference to these petty goings-on, and up came Brunnhilde's next cue: 'Ach, mein Vater' (Oh, my father) she sang, and then Manhattan took over from Valhalla again: 'Ah, the hell with it!' she cried, and after an impressive wind-up, hurled the spear into the wings of the Royal Opera House with all the force and accuracy of an Olympic javelin thrower.

The whole audience gasped in ecstatic shock, half expecting an innocent member of the chorus or the stage-crew to stagger onstage and fall flat on his face with eight feet of spear projecting from his back. It was not to be, but even without that half dreaded, half longed-for climax it was still a wildly exhilarating moment. I felt like giving her the sort of ovation the Cambridge undergrads had given me, but good manners and the importance of the occasion prevailed, and I contented myself with silently hugging Ernst (who was weeping with the effort of not laughing) and gave Mme Harshaw an extra-special cheer when she took her curtain-call at the end of the Act.

The second of the Great Evenings I Have Spent with Richard Wagner was far less spectacular, but if anything even more endearing. We were at Sadler's Wells for the dress rehearsal of a new production of the *Mastersingers of Nuremberg*, directed (most beautifully) by my old boss from the Young Vic, Glen Byam Shaw. The role of Walther in *Mastersingers* is a tough one. He is the leading tenor, with all that that implies in a Wagner opera in terms of physical and vocal stamina. He also has to sing the Prize Song, which is the only number in the entire score that most people know; not only that, he has to sing it absolutely brilliantly because it is sung in a competition and, as the title implies, he has to win The Prize. And on top of all that he has to perform this feat at the end of the evening after singing his heart out for about four and a half hours. As I said – it's a tough one.

The Walther on this occasion was a regular at Sadler's Wells, the very popular Alberto Remedios, a fine tenor from Cyprus with a lovely ringing voice and a most engaging and lovable personality. No-one *ever* called him Alberto – he was universally and affectionately known as Bert. That evening, Bert sang wonderfully right from the start; he was still sounding as fresh as a daisy in the final scene four hours later, and was obviously looking forward with great relish to the Prize Song, the juicy cherry on top of the delicious cake he had been cooking all evening.

The Prize Song, as well as being ferociously difficult to sing, has a slightly tricky structure. Round about the middle of the first part of the glorious opening melody, a descending phrase takes the tune down, then down again, and we start exploring new territory. After several minutes of intriguing exposition and development that same opening melody is reprised, but this time, at the same middle point of the first part, instead of the descending phrase we have an ascending one, taking us not down but up and away into fresh fields and pastures new. Walther has to keep his wits about him to be certain which way to go.

Bert stepped up onto the stage-within-a-stage which had been built for the singing competition in the Town Square of Nuremberg, the orchestra played the two magical chords of C major which are the entire introduction to this beautiful song, and Bert launched confidently and thrillingly into the opening melody. As he approached the crucial point his eyes glazed over, the happy smile faded, and I could see him thinking: 'Do I take the High Road or the Low Road?' He hesitated for no more than a second or two, but that was long enough for *every* tenor in the chorus to burst joyfully into song and deliver the troublesome line helpfully – and beautifully – in Bert's direction to the tune of the descending phrase. Bert picked it up immediately, and with a beatific smile turned to the chorus, said, 'Thanks very much, fellas,' and powered on to the end of the number to receive an entirely predictable and well-deserved ovation from everyone – including, of course, all the tenors in the chorus.

Needless to say, Ernst and I were not aiming at Wagner – our sights were set somewhat lower, but they were definitely aimed in the direction of musical theatre. What do you do, though, when you are offered *Lady Windermere's Fan* by Oscar Wilde, *Major Barbara* by Bernard Shaw, *Colombe* by Jean Anouilh, *Figure of Fun* (*Bobosse*) by Andre Roussin, *RUR* by the brothers Capek, *A Doll's House* by Ibsen, *The Tempest* by Shakespeare, and a Christmas pantomime – *Cinderella* – with music by Sir Arthur Sullivan? You accept, that's what you do. Eight great parts in these eight great plays were offered to me by John Harrison, who had been an actor with me at Birmingham back in 1945, and was now Artistic Director of the Nottingham Playhouse. It was impossible to resist, and dreams of musical comedy stardom were put on hold. It was a glorious season: the late, great Robert Eddison was a superb Prospero, while Stella joined us halfway through the season and was a beautiful singing Ariel in *The Tempest* and a dashing Dandini in *Cinderella*.

This was Rep the way it used to be – not the luxurious monthly turnaround of Birmingham, but not the almost impossible weekly grind either. It's amazing what you can do in two weeks if you prepare well and work hard – each one of these major plays was rehearsed, designed and staged in two weeks while playing another production in the evenings. The actors were all supremely professional and production standards were amazingly high. Looking back now, when a production at the National Theatre or the RSC gets five or six weeks' rehearsal and a week of previews before its official opening, it seems impossible, but it worked. We were all young, strong and enthusiastic, we played to full houses, and the regulars came to every production every season. The most amazing thing of all is that this went on all year round all over the country – not just in the major cities like Birmingham, Manchester, Bristol, Newcastle, Glasgow, but in every sizeable town from Amersham and Guildford to Burnley and Pitlochry.

The death of the live theatre has been confidently predicted time and again. The cinema was going to kill it off, but never quite managed it. The inexorable and universal spread of television was surely going to finish the job, but somehow, we're still here.

Chapter 5
Music, Ho!

IF BINKIE BEAUMONT was the King of the straight play in the West End, the smaller, slighter, but immensely popular little world of Intimate Revue was dominated for many years by Laurier Lister. The intimate revue, now virtually extinct, was a curious theatrical animal, part variety bill, part concert party, but aimed at a smarter and more sophisticated audience than those comparisons might suggest. Typically, half a dozen or so versatile actors would perform a series of sketches, songs and dances, with no perceptible common theme binding them together – a bit like an evening in Auntie Amy's Kitchen, really, but with a smaller cast. With very rare exceptions, the sketches were purely for laughs, usually with lots of slightly scandalous topical references. The songs were mostly in the same vein: every now and then there might be a 'charming' number, or even a 'moving' one, but overall the mood was one of light-hearted and often very witty satire, set to music of surprisingly high quality. Writers like Eleanor and Herbert Farjeon, Joyce Grenfell, Michael Flanders and Harold Pinter all contributed material over the years, as did composers of the stature of Noël Coward, Donald Swann and Richard Addinsell. It was undemanding, easy-going after-dinner entertainment, but it was most professionally crafted.

At any given moment there would usually be at least one intimate revue running in the West End. They tended to have rather twee titles, such as *Share my Lettuce, Intimacy at Eight*, or *Sweet and Low*, which had a sequel *Sweeter and Lower* and, I do believe, a sequel to *that* called *Sweetest and Lowest*. So when Laurier Lister came up with *Airs on a Shoestring* it sounded like a promisingly witty title, and I was tempted to audition for it. I read, I sang, and (after a fashion) I danced, and somewhat to my surprise Laurier took me on. 'I enjoyed your acting and singing very much,' he said. 'And don't worry, the ensemble dance routines will be very simple.' What tact.

The stars of *Airs on a Shoestring* were the talented up-and-coming Betty Marsden and the magnificent Max Adrian, absolute master of the art of acerbic yet genial satirical comedy. His Dauphin in Olivier's film of *Henry V* was definitive – an object lesson in clarity, nervous energy and wit. In our revue he appeared (among other manifestations) as a hooded fiend selling charity flags ('Ghoul's Day, Ghoul's Day; please spare a penny, it's Ghoul's Day'), as a fly cheerfully polluting a slice of salmon ('Excuse me, I must fly') and as an Everest-climbing sherpa who couldn't stand heights.

My own contributions were more modest and less startling, but besides being in several sketches and ensemble numbers I did actually have two solo songs. Admittedly both of them featured Moyra Fraser doing rather fetching dance numbers, and it goes without saying that more attention was being paid to her long, elegant, fishnet-clad legs than to my vocal accompaniment, but nevertheless there I was, singing solo on the London stage for the very first time, and loving it.

Airs on a Shoestring played at the Royal Court in Sloane Square, the theatre which George Devine had always wanted as the base for his newly formed English Stage Company, whose policy was to be the staging of new plays by contemporary English playwrights. The ace that George had up his sleeve was *Look Back in Anger*, a new play by an unknown young writer called John Osborne. Oscar Lewenstein, who was running the Royal Court, was most enthusiastic about George's plans, and promised him that the theatre was his as soon as it became available. There was just this little revue going on now called *Airs on a Shoestring*, which would only last a few weeks, and then the English Stage Company would be able to claim its rightful home. Unfortunately the little revue ran and ran, and poor George had to wait in the wings tearing his hair out for nearly two years before he could move in, stage *Look Back in Anger*, and change the face of the English theatre.

Ronald Searle was a great artist who was taken prisoner by the Japanese in Burma during the Second World War. He first sprang to fame with a masterly series of harrowing but beautiful drawings which survive as an indelible record of that terrible experience, but of course he reached an infinitely wider audience when he harnessed his wicked but affectionate sense of humour to create the immortal schoolgirls of St Trinian's. Somewhere in between those two extremes he plied his trade as the theatre cartoonist for *Punch* magazine. Every week the critic's review of a new production in the West End was adorned by a beautiful drawing which always captured the essence of the play – witty, elegant, perceptive and unmistakably Searle. A man of many parts then, an artist for all seasons, but until Wendy Toye twisted his arm he had never dreamed of being a set-designer for the theatre.

Wild Thyme, written by actor-turned-playwright Philip Guard, was a charming fairy-tale about the improbable romance between a young railway porter (me) and a mature French film star (Betty Paul). Stella was a cockney hiker, Donald Swann wrote some delightful songs, and Ronnie Searle's intimate and eccentric line drawings somehow blossomed into exuberant three-dimensional dream landscapes – a railway platform, a village pub, and a caravan in a field populated by floppy-eared rabbits who popped up through trapdoors like cuddly little Demon Kings. This slight but enchanting confection lasted for six weeks in a heatwave – not exactly a record-breaking run, but it did pick up some excellent reviews, especially (dare I say it) for me, and I was launched as a young leading man in the West End.

Around this time an apparently inexhaustible stream of vibrant and colourful American musicals were following the trail blazed by *Oklahoma!*, and landing spectacularly on our shores: shows like Rodgers and Hammerstein's *South Pacific*, Frank Loesser's wonderful *Guys and Dolls* and Leonard Bernstein's even more wonderful and beautiful *West Side Story*. Compared to these dynamic masterpieces most English musicals in the '50s looked rather pale and genteel.

There is an irresistible mixture of raw energy, high spirits and an almost child-like directness of emotion in the best of American theatre, which I personally find hugely stimulating, both to watch and to perform. When I was younger, of course, my taste for American writing and acting was formed entirely in the cinema. Rough but warm-hearted characters like Henry Fonda, Gary Cooper, Robert Preston and the great Spencer Tracy, the awesome grace and athleticism of Fred Astaire, Gene Kelly and Donald O'Connor, the tough sweetness and heart-rending singing of Frank Sinatra, the sublime partnership of Bob Hope and Bing Crosby, and more recently the great triumvirate of Kirk Douglas, Burt Lancaster and Paul Newman – all these have enriched my life and, I think, helped to add vigour and colour to my own work.

When I joined the National Theatre at the Old Vic with Laurence Olivier in 1970 (the beginning of a five-year spell of total fulfilment and enchantment), I worked in a dozen or more great plays by Shakespeare, Chekhov, Sheridan, Eduardo de Filippo – one great master after another, yet the two plays I remember with the most excitement and affection were both American – *The Front Page* by Ben Hecht and Charles MacArthur, and *Long Day's Journey into Night* by Eugene O'Neill.

But more of this later – I digress, as I often do. Back in the '50s, a little of the magic of those visiting American shows rubbed off on a British-born musical with the jaunty title *Grab Me a Gondola* – it was inspired by a hilarious real-life incident in which Diana Dors (a big film star of her day) led a posse of British stars and starlets to the Venice Film Festival, turned up for a press conference wearing a mink bikini, and arranged for somebody to push her into the Grand Canal. The resulting shots of her in mid-air heading for the Canal's murky waters with the Doge's Palace in the background hit all the front pages of the popular press and made her one of the most familiar faces (and bodies) in the world.

The vivacious Joan Heal reincarnated Mme Dors on stage and I played opposite her as a tough showbiz reporter called Tom Wilson. One London theatre critic whose first name was Tom and another whose surname was Wilson each claimed that the character was based on himself. I let them both believe it.

Grab Me a Gondola had a witty book by Julian More, good songs by Jimmy Gilbert, and some lovely dancing, but the best thing, the most marvellous thing about it, was that it ran on Shaftesbury Avenue for two years, and paid me the incredibly lavish salary of £50 a week, thereby making it possible for me to put down the deposit on a big, beautiful house overlooking Hampstead Heath, which has been home to Stella and me, three children, three grandchildren, Stella's mother, and a succession of friends, au pair girls, and flat-coated retrievers during the forty-odd years we have lived in its spacious, welcoming, high-ceilinged, big-windowed and untidy rooms.

In one of those rooms in 1958, my old friend Alexander Faris, conductor of Gilbert and Sullivan for d'Oyly Carte, composer of the immortal *Upstairs, Downstairs* theme, orchestrator for Pavarotti, author of a definitive biography of Offenbach – (I could go on) –

was listening with me to the Broadway cast recording of Leonard Bernstein's operetta *Candide*. We played it straight through without a break, spellbound. At the end we vied with each other for superlatives – such wit, such beauty, such energy – until finally I said: 'Sandy, this is one of the most exciting scores I've ever heard. Wouldn't it be wonderful if I could sing *Candide* and you could conduct it!'

A wildly improbable scenario, of course, but it happened.

When the West End production was set up for 1959, the London producers, to my incredulous delight, asked me to play Candide; but Bernstein of course had never heard of me, and the role had been played in New York by Robert Rounseville, a well established operatic tenor. Not surprisingly, Lenny wanted to know what he was letting himself in for, so he asked me to record an audition tape and send it to him in New York. He wanted two numbers from the show, one fast, one slow (a regular audition routine). Sandy Faris rehearsed the numbers with me and accompanied me on the piano for the recording. We sent the tape off to New York and sat biting our nails for a few days. Then a Western Union telegram arrived, sent to me personally at my Hampstead address. I tore it open and read 'SQUISITO, YOU HAVE THE PART, BERNSTEIN'.

I should have kept it, of course, framed it and hung it on the wall, but typically, I lost it. It's probably still mouldering away in a shoe-box somewhere in the attic or the basement, along with other irreplaceable memorabilia which any properly organised person would have filed neatly away for instant access, but which I despair of ever finding again. The sad thing is, of course, that I worry that people don't believe me when I tell them the story. But I have a very good memory for lines and those were the exact words. Oh, and yes – Sandy conducted it.

Bernstein's *Candide* is based on Voltaire's satirical novel of that name, in which our innocent and trusting young hero is beset by one disaster after another as he whizzes round the world in search of (among other things) the Meaning of Life. He is constantly buoyed up by his tutor Dr Pangloss's dictum that 'All's for the best in this best of all possible worlds'. So profoundly does Candide believe this (until his final disillusionment) that even when his home is destroyed and his entire family slaughtered, he sings:

My world is dust now
And all I loved is dead.
Oh let me trust now
In what my master said:
There is a sweetness
In ev'ry woe
It must be so
It must be so.

Unfortunately the show's book did not live up to that neat little lyric by Richard Wilbur, nor to Bernstein's scintillating score. It was written by Lillian Hellman, a great playwright and a great woman, one of the inspirational leaders of the fight-back against the infamous McCarthy trials, which were still a recent and vivid memory. She had been a member of Harold Clurman's famous Group Theatre in New York, as had the show's director, Bobby Lewis. The Group Theatre was very serious and very method-orientated; Hellman had never seen a musical in her life, and had no intention of seeing one now, thank you very much. She came up with a book which was, of course, beautifully written, and had many moving moments, but which completely lacked the light-footed, quick-witted and fast-moving style which Voltaire's picaresque masterpiece demanded.

Our director Bobby Lewis, of course, knew Lillian Hellman very well, and had a clause in his contract in big red day-glo capital letters stating that she was not to be allowed anywhere near rehearsals until the day before the opening night. Obediently, she turned up from New York on the appointed day, and came to see the final preview.

The next morning (the day of the opening) she and I were in a taxi together on our way to the BBC at Broadcasting House to give an interview. As we turned into Regent's Park she stopped chatting about the weather and how gorgeous London looked in the spring, and said:

'Honey, you know that last scene?'

'Yes, Lill – Miss Hellman.'

'Well, I want you to play it twenty years older, freezing cold, and cut out the tears.'

As we rounded Park Crescent my jaw went slack, and I said something like:

'Er, er...'

'What's the matter honey – you have a problem with that?'

'No, no, not a problem exactly. Miss Hell – er, Lill – I'm just wondering how much I can change between now and the opening this evening, especially as I shan't see the director until –'

She cut in on me halfway down Portland Place:

'Honey, I'm not asking you to *change* anything – just play it twenty years older, freezing cold, and cut out the fucking tears.'

I stumbled out of the cab in front of the beautiful, curved, pillared West Front of All Souls Church, Langham Place, opposite Broadcasting House, thinking: 'Thank you, Bobby, for keeping her out of rehearsals.'

The first night went quite well (no – I didn't change the last scene) and the applause at the final curtain, though not ecstatic, was warm and friendly until a rather half-hearted little burst of booing came out from a few people in the Dress Circle. When my friend script-writer Ian Kennedy Martin came to my dressing-room after the show to say hello, I said:

'Pity about the booing.'

'Oh, that was Sandy Wilson's party from *Valmouth*,' said Ian.

'No, no, no,' I laughed. 'Actors don't do that to fellow-actors.'

'I was there,' he replied, 'I saw them.'

A little explanation is called for here: Sandy Wilson, author-composer of one great hit show, *The Boy Friend*, had written a follow-up called *Valmouth*. It opened at the Lyric Theatre, Hammersmith, and did very well there. Sandy badly wanted to transfer it to the West End but couldn't find a theatre that was free, and was getting desperate. As a great favour, the producers of *Candide* offered him the Saville Theatre on Shaftesbury Avenue for a short time. They had booked the Saville for the opening of *Candide* in about six weeks, and as it was free until then, he could put *Valmouth* there until we came in, and then of course he would have to move. Sandy naturally grabbed the opportunity, and happily moved *Valmouth* in. It performed only moderately well because, in truth, the Saville, a great square barn of an ex-cinema (today, indeed, a cinema again) was much too big for such a small, intimate show. So, after six weeks *Valmouth* moved out, *Candide* moved in, we had our first night, our little bit of booing, and a quite respectable press the next morning. The following Sunday I choked on my breakfast toast and passed the *Observer* to Stella, saying: 'Tell me I'm not seeing what I think I'm seeing there.' She read it and said: 'I'm afraid you are.' Among the letters to the Editor I had read this:

> *Sir, I have never, to my knowledge, been classed as an Angry Young Man: but I'm very Angry today. Your latest guest critic,*

Harold Clurman, bends over backwards to find some merit in the newest American musical import 'Candide'; quite recently two of your theatre critics, the professional one (Tynan) and the amateur (Angus Wilson) took great pains to point out the faults in a British musical, my own 'Valmouth'. They seemed to know more about Ronald Firbank than Firbank knew himself, and as result of their criticism my show suffered.

That is one of the hazards of the Theatre, and I must accept it. But I'm darned if I'm going to accept an American Director's Flattery of an American travesty which has been foisted on Shaftesbury Avenue, having already failed on Broadway.

Of course some established names are involved: Lillian Hellman has contributed a witless, boring book; Robert Lewis has directed without a vestige of style or imagination; Jack Cole has tossed on some dances which even he must be shamed of; Osbert Lancaster has designed sets and costumes of breathtaking ugliness and ineptitude, outdoing even the horrors of 'Zuleika'; Leonard Bernstein has composed a pretty and amusing score. The whole thing is performed, for the most part, with a graceless exaggeration which would have earned any member of the casts of 'Valmouth' or 'The Boy Friend' the sack.

Tynan and A. Wilson maintained that I had missed the spirit of Firbank; But I'm glad to say that his family told me he would have loved the show. What about the spirit of Voltaire? Unfortunately he has no close living relatives to rise in a body and burn the Saville Theatre to the ground.

Sandy Wilson

I now believed Ian's story about the booing.

Donald Albery, who had now succeeded Binkie Beaumont as the most powerful theatrical management in the West End, had previously rung asking me to take over from Keith Michell as the male lead opposite Elizabeth Seal in a hugely successful musical called *Irma la Douce*.

'Sorry, Donald,' I had said, rather grandly; 'I'm about to play the title role in *Candide*, and I won't be available for a while.'

So Donald had engaged John Neville, and then some nine months later, as *Candide* was ending its run, he rang again to say that John was unhappy in the role and wanted to leave, and would I take over from him? I replied, even more grandly than before:

'You know Donald, a first take-over is one thing, but a *second* take-over – well really! In any case, I'm doing this wonderful American comedy called *Bachelor Flat*, which is going to keep me tied up for *quite* a long time.'

'OK, chum,' said Donald and rang off.

Bachelor Flat played its pre-London tour mostly in the north of England, and was an absolute riot – huge laughs, storms of applause, and ovations at the curtain-calls. Then we brought it in to the Piccadilly Theatre and went through the most agonising first night any of us had ever experienced. Lines which had got delighted belly-laughs in Newcastle, Manchester and Leeds dropped into pools of icy silence, and after two and a half hours of this, the curtain-call released us from our torment with a spattering of scattered hand-claps, drowned by the banging of seats going up as the punters got out of there as quickly as they could.

The reviews next morning were the stuff of nightmares. There was nothing particularly witty, such as 'Me No Leica' which was one Broadway critic's review of *I am a Camera*, or 'Katherine Hepburn runs the gamut of emotions from A to B,' another Broadway gem, but in their own, less flamboyant way, the London critics made it quite clear that we had blown it.

When I arrived in my dressing-room for the second night, the phone rang and a lady's voice said: 'I have Mr Albery for you.'

Donald came onto the line and said:

'Well, chum?'

Trying not to laugh or cry, I said:

'I'll be there on Monday.'

Bachelor Flat closed on the Saturday, so that was no problem.

Peter Brook, the callow youth who had directed me in my very first season at Birmingham back in 1945, was now, fifteen years later, one of the most successful directors in England, and poised to become one of the most revered theatre practitioners in the world, with his daring, improvisational productions at the Bouffes du Nord in Paris, and his renowned multi-national company which toured all over the world in every possible kind of venue – a quarry, a field, an amphitheatre – wherever there was a space he would fill it.

However, he had *en passant* found time to direct *Irma la Douce*. Obviously musicals were not his regular fare, but *Irma la Douce* was no ordinary musical. Written by a wild, free-spirited, chain-smoking, piano-bashing middle-aged French lady called Marguerite Monnot, it was set in a Paris bar frequented by a gang of endearing Parisian low-lifes and the tough but (of course) tender-hearted street-walker, Irma. The music was pure Paris – the Paris of Edith Piaf, Charles Trenet and Yves Montand – altogether an atmosphere so totally, irredeemably French that you would think it impossible to make it viable for an English audience without completely anglicising it, thereby destroying its essential character.

Top left: Cliff, DQ's father; Ada, DQ's mother. (Dates unknown.)
Top right: DQ's sister Jean ('Paddy') with DQ, late 1930s.
Bottom: DQ (seated third from left) at Bancroft's School, early 1940s.

I

Top: Abbas Mohammed el Hassan, baby Ahmed and DQ in Khartoum, 1947.
Bottom left: DQ in *The Lady from the Sea*, 1945.
Bottom right: DQ in publicity postcard for *The Black Arrow*, 1950.

Top left: DQ and SQ in *Lady's Not for Burning*, 1950. *Top right:* DQ and SQ wedding, 1950.

Bottom: DQ, Peter Reeves, Max Adrian, Charles Ross and Bernard Hunter in 'Guide to Britten' from *Airs on a Shoestring*, 1953.

Above: DQ and Jane Wenham in *Wild Thyme*, 1955.

IV

Top: DQ and Wendy Toye discussing *Wild Thyme*, 1955.
Bottom: DQ and Laurence Naismith in *Candide*, 1959.

Above: DQ (twice) in publicity shot for *Irma La Douce*, early 1960s.

Top: DQ in *Much Ado about Nothing*, 1963.

Bottom: DQ and Bob Monkhouse in *Boys from Syracuse*, 1963.

Top: DQ and Cicely Courtneidge (right) in *High Spirits*, 1964.
Bottom: DQ on set of *Contrabandits*, late 1960s.

© John Pearson

Photographer unknown/The Age

Top: DQ with Sarah and Joanna in Australia, late 1960s.
Bottom: DQ and June Bronhill posing as *Robert and Elizabeth*, 1966.

Top left: DQ in Australia, late 1960s. *Top right:* DQ as *The Entertainer*, 1969.
Bottom: Richard Burton (left) and DQ (right) in *Anne of the Thousand Days*, 1969.

Top: DQ, Leonard Rossiter and Cherith Mellor in *The Resistible Rise of Arturo Ui*, 1969.
Bottom: DQ and Anthony Hopkins in *Coriolanus*, 1971.

Top: DQ, Laurence Olivier, Constance Cummings, Ronald Pickup and Michael Blakemore in rehearsal for *Long Day's Journey into Night*, 1971.

Bottom: Laurence Olivier and DQ in *Long Day's Journey into Night*, 1971.

Top left: DQ in *A School for Scandal*, 1972. *Top right:* DQ and Ronald Pickup in *Richard II*, 1972.

Bottom: Constance Cummings, DQ and Michael Hordern in *The Cherry Orchard*, 1973.

Top: DQ, David Ryall and James Hayes in *The Front Page*, 1972.

Bottom: Albert Finney and DQ in a public performance on the South Bank, 1976.

Top: Albert Finney, Angela Lansbury and DQ (as the Ghost) in *Hamlet*, 1976.
Bottom: DQ (as Claudius) and Simon Ward in *Hamlet*, 1976.

Above: Laurence Olivier's leaving party, 1973: DQ, Joan Plowright, Laurence Olivier.

But Julian More, who translated and adapted it, somehow managed to preserve all the Gallic flavour while making it easily and charmingly accessible to English ears.

Peter Brook brought to it all the visual flair and musical sensibility which he had displayed all those years ago, but now supported by years of practical experience. The result was very beautiful, with sumptuous effects achieved by the simplest of means, and the tricky mixture of farce and bittersweet romance effortlessly controlled. Indeed for my taste what he achieved in this production and in his famous 'White Box' *Midsummer Night's Dream* was more imaginative, evocative and satisfying than some of the more self-consciously 'significant' work of his later years, when he had become a guru worshipped by awe-struck genuflecting pilgrims.

I spent a highly enjoyable nine months on Shaftesbury Avenue as Nestor-le-Fripé (Nestor the Shabby one) falling in love with his little street-walker, while outside in the real world, real street-walkers patrolled the pavements of the fringes of Soho behind the respectable Shaftesbury Avenue theatres. Each one had her own beat, and the stretch of pavement leading to our Stage Door was the territory of a really rather sweet and attractive girl (quite an exception to the general rule). She was always there when I arrived at the Stage Door each evening, and as the weeks went by we developed a pleasant, friendly relationship. We would nod and smile, wish each other good evening and enquire after each other's health. She knew what my job was, I knew what hers was, and we both enjoyed our little encounters.

She was not usually there when the show finished, but one night as I came out after the performance, I saw her walking a few yards ahead of me with her back to me. As I came up behind her she heard my footsteps and turned, saying:

'Hallo dear, would you like a nice – oh, I'm sorry, I didn't realise it was you.' She looked down at her feet and blushed. I was absurdly touched, and said:

'That's all right – don't worry.'

'No, no, I'm sorry,' she said again, and walked quickly away. It was a while before we could recapture our easy camaraderie but we managed it in the end.

Meanwhile, *Irma la Douce* had been playing very successfully for some months in New York as well as London, and whispers began to reach my keenly attentive ears that Keith Michell might be thinking of leaving the cast and coming home. The possibility that this opened up was almost too good to be true. I put it from my mind and concentrated on the job in hand; I told myself that I was doing too useful a job in Shaftesbury Avenue for Donald Albery to consider such a major upheaval. Much easier to leave me where I was, and find somebody new to replace Keith on Broadway.

I was sitting in my dressing-room making-up for a matinée when the phone rang. That familiar lady's voice trilled that familiar line: 'I have Mr Albery for you.' On came Donald: 'Well, chum – how do you fancy a trip to New York?'

Chapter 6
O, my America, my new-found land!

I SUPPOSE the best way to arrive in New York is (or was) on a luxury ocean liner, steaming past the Statue of Liberty, throwing paper streamers onto the dock and all that '30s jazz, but the next best way must be to jump into a yellow cab at JFK airport and make sure the driver understands enough English to take the route over the Queensboro Bridge. As you approach the bridge from the south, the view across the East River of the brutal, beautiful Manhattan skyline is simply heart-stopping: you are close enough to make out the quirky characteristics of individual buildings, but far enough away to see the cityscape as a whole, as it gradually rolls past you from Madison Square past the UN building to Central Park like a gigantic Cinemascope tracking-shot.

When you disembark exhausted in Midtown, the energy in the air hits you between the eyes like the blast of hot air that greets you as you step out of an aeroplane into the sunshine of a Caribbean island.

Revitalised and super-adrenalated, we embarked on a week or so of sightseeing: the Empire State Building, of course, and all the other not-to-be-missed places, like proper tourists; then up to the 70s for the magnificent Frick Collection, housed in a beautiful, serene, cloistered mansion which was once the home of the eponymous Mr Frick; and best of all, dinner at the 'Top of the Sixes,' a sumptuous restaurant on the top floor of number 666 Fifth Avenue with staggering views of the whole southern half of Manhattan island, from the Park and the Rockefeller Centre past Greenwich Village and all the way down to Brooklyn Bridge and the Battery Park. If you got yourself a window seat at the right time of day, you would see the sun begin to set sometime between the Rib-eye Steak and the Aunt Mary's apple pie à la mode, and then as the coffee was arriving, all the lights in all the buildings of the city sprang into life one after another, until everything down there below you was twinkling like the biggest and most beautiful Christmas tree you ever dreamed of as a child. And you were the fairy on top of the tree.

After all this over-excitement it was time to move out of our hotel room and get somewhere to live. We soon found a pleasant little apartment on the second floor of a typical old New York brownstone on East 63rd Street between Park Avenue and Madison Avenue. There was a small balcony at the back looking over a tiny but leafy garden, and a five-minute stroll took us to the Zoo entrance of Central Park, where there was a seriously good cafeteria – very handy for alfresco breakfast on a warm morning.

Apart from the cafeteria, the other great thing about Central Park was Joe Papp and his wonderful free outdoor productions of Shakespeare. To my ear, the American voice is ideally suited to Shakespeare's language. The accent is in many respects very similar to the West Country voices of those first pilgrims who sailed from Plymouth to New England, and from a great deal of internal evidence plus a fair bit of conjecture, students of language have come to the firm conclusion that this accent, or something very close to it, was how English was spoken, not just in the West Country but all over southern England, including London. In other words, Burbage and Will Kempe, Shakespeare himself and all the actors at The Rose and The Globe almost certainly spoke with an accent much closer to present-day American than to present-day English. Also, those American qualities of vigour, simplicity and directness of utterance, which I celebrated in an earlier chapter, are precisely the qualities which abound in the greatest Elizabethan writing. Surely they were meant for each other.

We saw Papp's production of *Richard II*, in which the actor playing Richard seemed to be doing his best to sound English, but came across as a pale imitation of John Gielgud with all the life, meaning and emotion drained out of the lines. The Bolingbroke, on the other hand (J D Cannon, if memory serves), used his own forceful, authoritative voice, his own native inflections and his own instinctive and intelligent response to the sense and rhythm of the lines, and as a result his character sprang to rugged but subtle life, and filled the big open-air arena with effortless power. When I played Bolingbroke myself at the Old Vic ten years later, I heard his voice clearly in my mind's ear.

New York of course is a place of wild contrasts: on the one hand the most open-hearted friendliness and generosity, on the other, rudeness of absolutely championship quality. One Saturday morning, shortly after I had opened in *Irma la Douce*, we dropped into the little art gallery and shop on the corner of our street to buy a few prints and posters to brighten up our walls. As we browsed, the owner said:

'You folks are from England, right?'

We couldn't deny it.

'You know my favourite place in the world? Bournemouth, England. When I retire that's where I'll go – Bournemouth, England.'

We chatted amicably about this and that, and as we were paying our bill and preparing to leave he said:

'What are you guys doing tomorrow?'

Tomorrow being Sunday, the answer was Not a Lot.

'Why don't you come out to my place on Long Island for a barbecue lunch?'

Quite taken aback by this instant offer after perhaps fifteen minutes of acquaintance, we stammered delightedly that it sounded like a lovely idea.

'Great – I'll come and pick you up in the morning. What time?'

I explained that I had two performances that day, finishing round about 11pm, and wouldn't be getting up very early on Sunday morning.

'Oh, you're in the theatre – OK, great. What – 11 o'clock, 11.30, 12 noon? – you name it.'

We settled on 11.30 and gave him our address. Promptly at 11.30 on Sunday morning a car toot-tooted outside, and there he was with his two children, and off we went to Long Island. His wife Audrey ('Call me Aud') greeted us like long-lost friends, we had a delicious barbecue and lazed in the garden talking till early evening, when he drove us back home.

His name was Marvin Pocker and he was an absolute gentleman. After we left the States he visited London two or three times, and each time he insisted on taking us out to dinner at the Mirabelle, his 'favourite restaurant in the world'. Then we lost touch. I wonder if he ever realised his dream of settling down in Bournemouth, England? Sadly, I fear not – I think we would have heard.

The following Sunday was one of those stiflingly hot New York days when all the air-conditioners in town are humming and dripping outside the buildings all day, and the women in the streets are wearing bare-shouldered cotton dresses and carrying dinky little angora sweaters which they put on every time they venture inside to brave the sub-zero temperatures in every store, bar or restaurant.

We had been for a very gentle morning stroll in the Park, and arrived, sweating, at the South side, heading for the St Moritz Hotel, which had a pavement café rather grandly called the Café de la Paix – a handful of tables under umbrellas out on the sidewalk, just the place for a cool drink after our exertions. I was wearing, as any sane man would on such a day, a nice clean short-sleeved shirt and a neat pair of cotton trousers – I thought I was looking rather elegant, actually. I approached the Maître d' (resplendent in red monkey-jacket and black bow tie) and said, 'Excuse me –' I was planning to say, 'Excuse me, is this table taken?' because one of the chairs was tipped in against it, but I got as far as 'Excuse me –' and he took a look at me and barked:

'You need a jacket!'

I went very English, fixed him with what I hoped was a withering eye and said:

'I see. In that case thank you *very* much and good *morning*.'

As we walked away he yelled along the sidewalk to my retreating back:

'*And* a necktie!'

The friend we were walking with shrugged his expressive Jewish-American shoulders and said, with a wry smile:

'Welcome to Noo York.'

A few days later we took in a baseball game at the Yankee Stadium: all good clean fun with lots of shouting, beer drinking and abuse of the umpires (just like home!) but fabulously skilful players and a thrilling and fascinating game. At half-time I headed for the hot-dog stall, which consisted of one man up on a circular dais with a hot-box full of a whole lot of frankfurters and buns. By the time I got there he was surrounded on all sides by big, sweaty men standing about four deep, all waving dollar bills and shouting 'Gimme one,'

'Gimme four' and in one really exciting case 'Gimme eight!' (A family of four, perhaps? Two dogs each?) And there I was standing shyly at the back, waving my hand and saying rather diffidently (but of course with splendidly resonant voice-production thanks to Ernst Urbach):

'Could I have two, please?'

His head swiveled round as if pulled by a string, he looked at me with an astonished expression and said:

'What was that?'

Slightly embarrassed by now, having become the centre of all attention, I mumbled:

'Er, two, please?'

A radiant smile lit up his face, he reached over the heads of the crowd and pressed two into my hand, saying:

'You said please, you're gonna have 'em right away. You enjoy the game now.'

I did too.

Success is crucial in the Big Apple. Or rather the perception of success – if you are not actually successful yourself you must associate with those who are, and if possible be seen doing so. I used not to believe the stories of guests at a Broadway first night leaving the after-show party when bad reviews started to arrive, but one night in Sardi's (*the* restaurant for theatre people) I was there when it happened.

The supper party was in full swing, the two stars were at a big table surrounded by friends and well-wishers, the champagne was flowing and everyone was having a great time. Then, at about 1am a man looked in at the door and held up one hand with the thumb and all four fingers pointing downwards. This meant five bad reviews. The atmosphere changed instantly; smiles disappeared, conversation became furtive and embarrassed, and very soon quite a lot of people finished their drinks and (in the immortal words of the *News of the World* reporter investigating 'Sex for Sale in London') made their excuses and left. We stayed much longer than we had intended, just to show solidarity.

On a very different evening, a friend of a friend, who had never met us but had heard that we were in town and living nearby, invited us to his apartment to meet a few neighbours. It was a pleasant occasion; we all circulated, as one does, introducing ourselves and chatting cosily about the weather and how the neighbourhood was going down, and eventually I found myself talking to a man who said:

'I hear you're from London, England – what are you doing over here?'

'I'm in *Irma la Douce* at the Plymouth Theatre.'

'Uh-huh,' he said, and after a little more desultory conversation we drifted apart.

I met him again at a similar gathering two or three days later. As I came into the room he cried:

'Hey – I've heard of British reserve, but this is *ridiculous*. Why didn't you tell me you were the leading *man* for Christ's sake!' Then he took me by the elbow for a tour of the room, saying: 'Hey, folks, this is Denis Quilley, he's the leading man in *Irma la Douce*,' and all the time I was thinking: 'Whoa – slow down. You don't know me any better or like me any more than you did a couple of days ago – you've just seen my name above the title outside the theatre, that's all.'

But hey, folks, I must admit it was very flattering.

My most enjoyable and dramatic moment of vicarious fame and success, however, took place (rather appropriately) at the Opera. We were at the City Centre to see *The Marriage of Figaro*, and were standing in the crowded foyer looking hopefully around for somewhere that might offer a drink, and perhaps a little space – New York theatres, surprisingly, tend to be even less well equipped in these areas than their London counterparts. Suddenly, over on the far side of the foyer, I saw Leonard Bernstein. (This was just a couple of years after the London production of *Candide*, which of course he had seen and greatly praised.) He was standing with his astrakhan-collared overcoat slung casually but elegantly over his shoulders, talking with two star-struck young men who hung adoringly on his every word. He turned in mid-flow to point out something on the wall above my head, and saw me. Our eyes met, recognition dawned and he sailed majestically across the room, the jam-packed crowd parting like the Red Sea before this charismatic, irresistible Moses; he opened his arms wide and with a dazzling smile cried, 'Denis! I don't believe it!' and engulfed me in a bear-hug and kissed me on both cheeks. About five hundred sophisticated opera-loving New Yorkers, who had been learnedly discussing Mozart and da Ponte, were suddenly all hissing to each other like old ladies peeping round their net curtains, and saying:

'Who's that? Who's that being kissed by Lenny Bernstein?'

And the little boy inside me was saying:

'Me, *me*, ME!'

It was worth crossing the Atlantic for.

We became very good friends with our two stage managers at the Plymouth Theatre, Woody Romoff and Murray Gitlin. When I first asked Murray where the name Gitlin came from he was very defensive.

'I'm American, I'm American,' he would say. Well, of course I knew he was American, but I was interested to know what his background was. He knew mine, after all. After a time, when we knew each better, he shyly revealed that it was a Russian name: his parents had emigrated to the States when he was a little boy, and in truth he was so nostalgic for his Russian home that he kept his grandmother's samovar in his kitchen, and the lamp which once burned in the bedroom he shared with his baby brother now stood in his own bedroom in Manhattan.

One day Woody and Murray decided to make a statement. They were both Jewish, and they were going to demonstrate to themselves, and to anyone else who cared to know that despite the war and the holocaust they harboured no ill-feelings against the Germans, and to prove it they were going to eat in a German restaurant. Woody told me the story.

'We went into this restaurant, Denis. Very comfortable, very elegant, nice smiling waiters. We sat down at the table and we ordered the first thing on the menu, knödel mit something or other – some kind of a soup with dumplings in it. It arrived, didn't look bad, didn't look bad at all. We picked up our spoons and forks, we bit into the dumplings, and simultaneously – *simultaneously*, Denis – two sets of thousand-dollar bridgework fell out of our mouths and into the soup. I looked at Murray and I said, "Murray, it's a sign from God," and we got up and we left and we're never going to eat in a German restaurant *ever* again!'

It was Woody and Murray who introduced me to Carmine Gagliardi. They took us to a restaurant called the Château Henri Quatre whose interior, true to its name, had been transformed into a really, really kitsch Disneyland Anglo-French Château, complete with drawbridge, portcullis and battlements, with *tricolore* banners flying at every corner. It was a wonder there was any room left for people to sit and eat. A very decent little four-piece band struck up, and on came a stocky middle-aged man of handsome Mediterranean appearance who, without any introduction or fuss, launched straight into 'Vesti la Giubba' from *I Pagliacci*.

He was magnificent. He had a robust, absolutely natural and relaxed tenor voice which he used with great charm and skill, very much in the Italian manner, like a slightly rough-hewn Pavarotti. His top notes rattled the fragile walls of the Château, his sobs at the end of the aria were heartrending, and he received a standing ovation, not least from me. He had two brothers, both of whom also had fine tenor voices. ('The Gagliardi Brothers' – what a great Vaudeville act that would have made. 'Eat your hearts out the Three Tenors!')

The Gagliardis had never had a single singing lesson between them, but Carmine, although entirely self-taught, was a teacher himself, and this was why meeting him was not just a pleasure, but the beginning of a really rewarding collaboration. I started taking lessons from him, and his forthright, extrovert Italian style was a stimulating contrast to Ernst Urbach's more inward and thoughtful approach. It didn't contradict Ernst's teaching, it complemented it, and helped me to find a more outgoing and uninhibited sound when singing on stage in a big theatre.

Mental images can be very useful to a singer: some work for one person, different ones for another, and some teachers have the most bizarre ideas for these images: to think of yourself vomiting, for example, or to picture the tone you are producing as a ping-pong ball balancing on a delicate little column of air or water. But Carmine came up with the one crucial image for me which I have used almost without thinking ever since.

I was talking to him about the importance of keeping the throat open and relaxed, and he suddenly barked:

'You haven't got a t'roat!'

'Sorry?'

'You haven't *got* a t'roat! You've got your bellows down here' (whacking his diaphragm) 'and your resonators up here' (stabbing his nose and forehead) 'and there is *nothing* in between!'

It worked immediately, and the exhilarating picture of the air whizzing straight up that unrestricted Italian autostrada and going 'Vroom, Vroom' in the front of my cranium has never let me down. I was reminded of another lovely breakthrough moment back at the Globe in *The Lady's not for Burning*, when John Gielgud sensed that, like many young actors, I was having trouble knowing what to do with my hands.

'Squilley, dear,' he said, 'try to think of your hands as two heavy weights hanging on strings at your sides, and then forget about them.'

Abracadabra! An instant and permanent cure – no more hand problems! Plenty of other problems, but not with the hands.

My dresser at The Plymouth was Charlie Blackstone, a tough, wiry little guy who had been a bit of boxer in his day, and now fancied himself as a bit of a trainer. Certainly he looked after me as if I were Mohammed Ali: on matinée days he would give me a punishing massage between shows finishing with an alcohol rub, a slap on the back, and:

'OK, champ, you're in great shape, now get out there and sock it to 'em.'

He introduced us to the innocent pleasures of the ten-pin bowling alley just down the block, and showed us precisely where to hit the front pin so that it fell at the right angle to hit the two in the second row, which would then hit the three behind, which in turn would hit the back four, and all ten would hit the deck with a satisfactory rattle like a burst of machine-gun fire, drowned by ecstatic cries of 'Strike!' We actually achieved this perhaps twice.

Charlie loved classy popular music, and his heroes were the same as mine – Frank Sinatra, Tony Bennett, Ella Fitzgerald, Louis Armstrong – and most nights, during the half hour of making-up and dressing before the show, we would duet our way through large swathes of the repertoire – a bit hazy on the lyrics sometimes, but right in there with the melodies. One night he arrived humming the great romantic theme from the last movement of Rachmaninov's second piano concerto.

'Hey, Charlie,' I cried in amazement. 'What's this, Rachmaninov?'

'Rack who?'

'That tune – it's by Rachmaninov.'

'No, no, champ, that's one of Brooks Benton's numbers,' and he raised his voice in song: 'Full moo-oon and empty a-armms ...'

That's all I can recall of the words, but I remember thinking it was really not a bad lyric for that luscious, swooning melody.

As the New York run of *Irma la Douce* began to draw to an end, plans were solidified for a major national tour – Boston, Chicago, Philadelphia, Milwaukee, San Francisco, Los Angeles, Washington and more. The prospect of spending a month or more in each of these archetypal American cities, whose names were so familiar to us from books and films but which we had never set eyes on, was dazzling. I was bursting with joyful anticipation.

A week or so before the end of the run Charlie came in looking an absolute picture of misery. He sat down and looked at the floor.

'Champ, I gotta tell you somethin'.'

'What is it Charlie? You look terrible – are you ill?'

'No, I'm OK. It's just ...'

'Come on, Charlie, what's wrong?'

He lifted up his head and looked me in the eye.

'I can't do the tour.'

I didn't know what to say. We were silent for a while.

'Why, Charlie?'

'You're goin' south of the line.'

'The line?'

'You know – Mason-Dixon?'

My memory clicked in. The Mason-Dixon Line is the border between Pennsylvania and Maryland, the theoretical and popularly accepted division between North and South.

'Mason-Dixon, champ. I'm not goin' South of the line. A black man is a second-class citizen down there.'

'But Charlie, you'll be with all of us in the Company, and we'll –'

'No, champ. I swore I'd never go South of the line. I can't go.'

There wasn't much singing as we prepared for the show that night.

But the very next night he turned up with what passed for a smile on his face. He had a friend who was free and would be happy to come on tour with us. He was a very good dresser and we would like him – he was a nice guy. He was right here in the theatre if I'd like to say hello? Of course, I'd love to say hello. He opened the door and beckoned, and Harry Watkins walked into the dressing-room and into our lives.

Where Charlie was short and stocky, Harry was tall and willowy. He had been a singer and dancer in his youth, and in middle age still had a dancer's grace of movement. He had spent most of his performing years in Paris, where black artists were not merely tolerated but celebrated, and treated like the stars they were, unlike America at that time, when Billie Holiday had to make her way to her dressing-room through the kitchens. He was billed as 'Harry Watkins, le Grand Chanteur du Jazz,' and the photos in his album showed a dashing young man in white tie and tails twirling elegantly with a girl on each arm, and in the background a pianist sitting at the obligatory white baby-grand.

Charlie was right – we did like Harry, he really was a nice guy, and he had the most beautiful, courtly manners. Even much later, when he and Stella and I had become close friends, he always addressed us as Mr and Mrs Quilley – not obsequiously, but with charming, friendly formality. We could not have had a more congenial companion on our Great American Voyage of Discovery.

The first impression of Boston in January was of bone-chilling, mind-numbing cold. The ten-minute walk from the hotel to the theatre was like an expedition to the North Pole, with Stella invisible inside layer upon thick woolly layer of insulation, and me very manly and British in my duffel-coat – all the rage among the casual younger set in '60s London, but a source of much curiosity and amusement for your average Bostonian. It took a good long blast of hyper-efficient American central heating, plus the glowing warmth of Harry's greeting as I staggered gratefully into the womb of my dressing-room, to thaw me out in time for my all acting, all singing, all fake-dancing turn on the stage every night.

But the city was beautiful: the State House up on Beacon Hill with its gilded dome looking over the Charles river; the tall slender spire of the Old North Church, nobly guarded by the statue of Paul Revere on his famous horse; the grand house where we had drinks with the British Consul-General in an enormous, beautiful room with a high oval ceiling, all elegant blue and white mouldings, like an exquisite and perfectly preserved piece of eighteenth-century London in the middle of twentieth-century Massachusetts. It somehow came as no surprise to learn that during the period just before and after the Civil War, Boston was the literary capital of America: Ralph Waldo

Emerson, Henry David Thoreau, Oliver Wendell Holmes, John Greenleaf Whittier, Henry Wadsworth Longfellow, and the best of them all (and the only one not sporting a grandiose middle name) Nathaniel Hawthorne, were all actively writing during those few remarkable years.

It was music, though, not literature, which, in two very different ways, made Boston memorable. Symphony Hall, a plain unpretentious building on Huntington Avenue, has superb acoustics (if only our Festival Hall in London had such warmth and resonance) and is home to the Boston Symphony Orchestra, one of the world's great bands. We managed to hear them a couple of times, and the precision, warmth and musicality of their playing was (of course!) even more stunning heard live than on record, which was the only way I had heard them until now. Thrilling, world class music-making.

Another great band, which was founded in Boston in that momentous January of 1962 had the following personnel: Stella Quilley, piano; Murray Gitlin, soprano recorder; Denis Quilley, alto recorder; and Woody Romoff, cello. We knew the boys played a bit in their spare time, and we had enjoyed a few impromptu sessions in New York when they visited us in our apartment (the only one with a piano) though living as we did in different areas of the city it never became a regular routine. But now that we had nine months or more to look forward to with all of us staying in the same hotels and having a fair amount of leisure during the day, the opportunity was too good to miss. We all went to the local music shop and rented a piano to go into our hotel suite; I bought a recorder to stand in for the flute I had left behind in London, then we thumbed through the sheet music and found lots of pleasant pieces, mostly Baroque – Handel, Purcell and so on, not too difficult to play and well suited to our ground-breaking little Early Music ensemble, with two top lines (Murray on the melody, me on the harmony), a keyboard part for Stella and a juicy, striding ground-bass for Woody's cello.

After some agonisingly awful first attempts we gradually got quite good, and it was so enjoyable that from then on I always phoned ahead to the next city on the tour, made sure we had a big enough suite in the hotel, and ordered a piano to be waiting for us when we arrived. Word got around the theatre, and once or twice we actually had half a dozen of the *Irma la Douce* company sitting on the floor of our hotel room and listening with most professionally sustained smiles of pleasure to what we bravely called a concert. Murray perches his stocky, muscular limbs incongruously on a dainty gilt chair, the little recorder even more incongruously raised to his lips; Woody, by contrast, looks every inch the cellist – thin frame bent narrowly over the instrument, greying black shock of hair falling over his forehead, glasses on the tip of his nose, waiting for Stella to start us off.

'One, two, three *and*,' she commands. Murray and I blow, Stella strums, and Woody cries, 'Wait, wait, WAIT!,' adjusts his chair, lengthens the spike of his cello, searches for the right position for his fingers, and says, 'OK – OK.'

'One, two, three *and* –' And we're off, with Purcell turning in his grave and the four of us having the time of our lives.

If I described walking across Boston in January as a Polar expedition, only Shakespeare can do justice to Chicago in February:

> .... to reside
> In thrilling region of thick-ribbèd ice;
> To be imprisoned in the viewless winds,
> And blown with restless violence round about Lake Michigan.

Yes, all right, I made up the last line – it actually reads 'round about the pendent world,' and this is Claudio in *Measure for Measure*. Coleridge comes a close second, even if his verse in this particular passage doesn't quite live up to his own highest standards:

> The ice was here, the ice was there,
> The ice was all around;
> It cracked and growled, and roared and howled
> Like noises in a swound.

Lake Michigan was frozen solid as far as the eye could see, and frozen snow-drifts were piled high on top of the very thick-ribbèd ice. And I think even the intrepid Ancient Mariner (for that was he, going on about noises in a swound) would have trembled in the face of the wind which roared across the frozen lake and whistled like Concorde all the way down Michigan Avenue, which fronts the lake from end to end. Would we ever feel warm?

Music did the trick again, as it always does. The awesome virtuosity of the Chicago Symphony Orchestra, the piercing sweetness of the strings and the blatant power of the brass, thawed us out miraculously. This was rapidly becoming a tour of Great Orchestras of the World. Boston and Chicago seen and heard, Cleveland and Philadelphia still to come.

'A large Scotch, please,' I said to the barman of our Cleveland hotel as we arrived late on Sunday evening, exhausted after two shows in another town the night before and a very long Sunday train journey.

'Three-two,' he replied.

'Um, no, double whisky, please.'

'Three-two, Mac, three-*two*!' He was getting a little impatient with this dumb Limey.

'What is this man saying to me?' I asked Woody.

'He is saying, Denis, that this being a Sunday, which is, as you may know, the Christian Sabbath,' he grinned wolfishly and raised a disapproving Jewish eyebrow.

'All right,' I interrupted. 'What were you doing yesterday, then, working two shows on *your* Sabbath?'

'This being a Sunday,' he reprised, trying not to laugh, 'the State of Ohio forbids you to drink anything stronger than beer with an alcohol content of 3.2 per cent.'

Ah, well, there was the great Georg Szell and the Cleveland Orchestra to come (absolute knock-out – three down, one to go) and there was Joe Bova's family to meet. Joe was playing Bob the barman on the hour, and he was the absolute embodiment of the young all-American male: Brooks Bros suit, button-down shirt, college tie and haircut, neat as a pin and bright as a button. Cleveland was his hometown, so we went to tea and met his father and grandfather.

Poppa Bova was a role that the great Hollywood character actor Joseph Calleia would have seized upon with relish: a larger-than-life cameo of a noisy, warm-hearted, irascible, emotional, lovable Italian-American, talking volubly in that ebullient accent which makes English sound like Italian opera sung in American – lovely to listen to but impossible to reproduce on the page without caricature – accompanied always, of course, by extravagant and intimidating gestures. He plainly adored his son and was immensely proud of his success in this American world which he had made his own.

Grandad was from another world again. He spoke not a word of English, nor did he speak standard Italian; his only language was a very strong Sicilian dialect in which I, with my smattering of 'normal' Italian, could only find a word or two here and there that I understood.

Poppa was the go-between, speaking English to us, occasional phrases of Italian to Joe, and Sicilian to Grandad, translating in both directions to keep things going. It was a potted history of three generations of immigration and assimilation – from Sicilian peasant to American college boy, all together in one room.

In Philadelphia (Great American Bands no. 4 – perhaps less brilliant than Chicago, but warmer, more romantic – you pays yer money…), in Philadelphia, Stella caught a bug and was prescribed some pills. She took them religiously but seemed to be getting worse, until one of the local stage-crew saw her backstage filling a glass from the tap to wash a pill down, and yelled:

'My God, what are you *doing*? You're not drinking the *water*? You can't drink the water in Philadelphia – it'll *kill* you! Why do you think we have all these *coolers* around the theatre?'

And indeed there they were, water-coolers dotted around at strategic points backstage and in the wings – we somehow hadn't taken much notice of them. Severely chastened, Stella used the coolers from then on and, magically, got better in no time. Now I know why Americans are so fussy about the water when they're abroad – they know what it's like at home.

Besides poisoning my wife, Philadelphia also hosted the out-of-town opening of a musical called *I Can Get it For You Wholesale*. Its star was Elliott Gould, who had been one of the boys in *Irma la Douce* with me on Broadway, and was now opening in his first ever leading role. He was quite brilliant, and was very soon launched on a big career on stage and screen.

Playing opposite him, in the supporting role of Miss Marmelstein,

(Miss Marmelstein
Miss Marmelstein

Why do they call me Miss Marmelstein?
My name is Sadie – Sa – adie)

was an unknown girl called Barbra Streisand. Not much of a singing voice, but a terrific acting performance and a personality that leapt out over the footlights. One of the producers threw an after-show party in his vast, luxurious apartment, and in the course of nosily poking our way around the various rooms (as one does) we stumbled upon the bathroom. It was enormous, of course, and absolutely everything in it was pink. The bath, the lavatory, the bidet, the walls, the floor, every one of the myriad pots of creams, lotions and unguents ranged along the shelves – all pink. And there, holding one of the pink pots to her formidable nose, was this little bird-like nineteen-year-old Miss Marmelstein from Brooklyn taking a deep ecstatic sniff. She looked up at us, half amused, half guilty, and said:

'Isn't this divine? Isn't it just di-*vine*? I'm gonna have a bathroom just like this one day.' She's probably got about twenty of them by now.

Not long afterwards, back in London, we heard her first album. The voice, of course, was absolutely stunning – it may not have rung any bells in the unforgiving space of a big live theatre, but put a microphone in front of her and she works miracles.

The main thing I remember about Washington is that when Jackie Kennedy came backstage after seeing the show she used my loo, and the *only* thing I remember about Milwaukee is a picture of Jesus. As well as our musical sessions with Murray and Woody, we had fallen into a routine in which Byron Mitchell, a handsome, charming member of the *Irma* company, would come to our suite at noon on the first Monday in each town and drink a welcoming vodka martini. The view from our window in Milwaukee was of a gigantic poster of

Jesus with his outstretched arms reaching literally from one end of the block to the other: it was the *entire* view – nothing else could be seen. Across the picture, in red letters about fifty feet high, ran the slogan: 'Jesus wants you. Are you ready?' Byron had picked up his martini and was just raising it to his lips when he glanced out of the window and saw the poster. He did a beautifully over-the-top double take, dismissed Jesus with an elegantly camp wave of his free hand, and said (with great bravado, but just a touch of nervousness?):

'Ask me tomorrow.'

His drink went down without touching the sides.

After a glorious month in San Francisco, whose beauties demand a whole chapter to themselves (perhaps another time?) we fetched up in Los Angeles, a town I have revisited since and have never quite been able to get to grips with. It was here that *Irma la Douce* and I finally parted company; the tour was continuing for some months, but I had served out my contract and we were both ready to go home. I played my last performance, we bade fond farewells to the company, swore eternal allegiance to Murray and Woody over a drink in the Green Room, then went back with Harry Watkins to my dressing-room to clear my things out and say our goodbyes to Harry. The clearing-out was easy: saying goodbye was harder. The three of us had forged a strong bond over the last nine months and parting was a serious wrench. Eventually, after hugs and kisses all round, we made it out to the waiting taxi. As I started to load my gear, Stella realised she had left her handbag behind and ran back to fetch it. I waited for what seemed a very long time, then went back in to see what had happened.

Harry was sitting in my make-up chair with tears streaming down his face, and Stella was kneeling at his feet holding his hand.

'I don't want you folks to go. Can't you stay? I don't want you to go.'

'We've got to go, Harry,' she was saying through her own tears. 'We've got our flight booked – we have to go back to London.'

'Well, can't you take me with you? I could work for you over there in London – take me with you.'

I couldn't speak – I was too upset, and I felt like an intruder. After a while I pulled myself together and joined in, and the three of us talked it through. Harry gradually composed himself and said of *course* he understood, and how *silly* of him to have imagined it could be any other way, and somehow – I can't remember how or when – we got out and into the cab and sat holding hands in silence all the way.

We stopped over in New York for a couple of days on the way to London, and I thought what the hell, let's stay at the Plaza. We got out of the cab at what I think must be my favourite spot in New York, with the Plaza sitting grandly on Central Park South, and the line of Hansom cabs waiting for custom behind the pretty little statue that looks down Fifth Avenue. It was early autumn, crisp and cool, and the windows of all the skyscrapers glinted bravely in the sunlight. Surely this was the most exciting town in the world.

'I would like a large double room, please, on a high floor looking over the Park.'

The very imposing but very kindly Frenchman manning the Front Desk looked me up and down with an experienced eye. I was dressed in old casual clothes, scruffy and rumpled from the long journey, and no doubt looked a bit young, and certainly not at all like a rich businessman.

'That will be ninety dollars, m'sieur,' he whispered – entirely without condescension – just a friendly warning. (And ninety dollars for a hotel room in 1962 merited a warning.)

'That'll be fine,' I said with a broad smile. 'Thank you very much.'

'And thank *you*, jeune m'sieur,' he smiled back, and handed me the key. We were on the top floor, and the view embraced the whole length of the Park and beyond, to the North of the Harlem river. It was worth every cent.

The following evening Leonard Bernstein was conducting the New York Philharmonic, and we pulled some strings to get in. He conducted the whole concert from memory, without score. Well, the opening piece was Copland's *Appalachian Spring*, which of course he knew backwards and could have conducted in his sleep. But next came a symphony by Roussel – by no means mainstream repertoire – which he could not have conducted many times before. Once again, no score, but every tempo change perfectly judged, every entry cue to individual sections clearly and confidently signalled – a formidable feat of memory. And so on through the whole evening, at the same time giving a positively balletic platform display to thrill the girls in the gallery.

A perfect farewell to the tough, tender, ugly, beautiful Isle of Manhattan, and to America, my new-found land. Next morning we were on the plane to London.

Chapter 7

It is the bright day that brings forth the adder

WE HAD SCARCELY set foot in London when I was asked to go back to New York. As I was unpacking my bags I learned that there had been a call from Ray Stark, a powerful theatre and film magnate now remembered, if at all, as Koo Stark's father: I was invited (commanded?) to drinks at the Dorchester. Without wishing to malign an august institution which I am *sure* has cleaned up its act in the intervening years, let me just coyly hint that I was now about to enjoy the front-of-house delights of an establishment whose slightly less luxurious backstage pleasures I had sampled in my heyday as a professional dishwasher.

Mr Stark and I sat comfortably drinking whisky and soda in his elegant, cockroach-free apartment, and he dangled temptations and dollar-signs before my eyes. He was putting on a musical called *The Fanny Brice Story*, loosely based on the life of that legendary Broadway comedienne, and the starring role was to be played by none other than Barbra Streisand, our little perfume-loving friend from the pink bathroom in Philadelphia. He needed a leading man to play opposite her as her lover Nick Arnstein, 'and what we're looking for, Denis, is a young Cary Grant who can sing.'

A young Cary *Grant*? *Moi*? 'Oh wad some Pow'r the giftie gie us, To see oursels as others see us!'

His blandishments got him nowhere, not even with the extra inducement of a second whisky and soda. We had just spent a tough year and a half in the States, and were in no mood to go whizzing straight back before our feet touched the ground. But the real clincher

114

was much more important – Sarah had arrived. Our first daughter, with bright blue eyes, and hair like a beautiful blonde brush.

The Fanny Brice Story became *Funny Girl*, was a huge hit on Broadway, made Streisand a star, and went on to be filmed with some young upstart called Omar Sharif as Nick Arnstein.

But we had other, more enjoyable fish to fry. The IRS (the American income tax office) has the excellent habit of extorting a 30% withholding tax from all visitors' earnings and then, when you leave the country, giving you a rebate (with a bit of luck and a good accountant) amounting to the difference between what you actually owe them and the 30% they have been holding.

In my case, after eighteen months on pretty high earnings, and with the help of an astute New York tax lawyer, the rebate was massive. We brought a very handy pile of US dollars back to London, a large part of which went towards installing central heating in our house. All those big, beautiful, high-ceilinged Victorian rooms were the devil to heat, and putting in a system big enough to cope with all of them cost a small fortune, but now we had not just a big livable and beautifully situated house, we had a *warm* house. *Grab Me a Gondola* paid for the house, *Irma la Douce* paid for the heating, and it was worth every penny.

Having achieved that, we then perversely took off for Spain, and drove the whole length of the Andalucian coast with six-month-old Sarah in the carry-cot. I soon discovered that, unlike England, where the sight of a baby automatically brings down the No Vacancy shutters over the receptionists' eyes, in Spain I had only to walk in with this little blonde-haired, blue-eyed beauty in my arms and enquire 'Hay un cuarto, por favor?' to be instantly surrounded by every cook, cleaner and chambermaid in the building. Hands were clasped in near-religious ecstasy, and amid adoring cries of 'Ah, que guappa!'

Sarah was gently but firmly prised from my arms and spirited away into the kitchens to be force-fed huge amounts of highly unsuitable food, while the smiling receptionist handed us the keys to the best room in the house.

Rodgers and Hart's 1938 musical *The Boys from Syracuse* had a successful revival in 1962 in a tiny off-Broadway theatre, and when it was decided to bring it to London the director, Chris Hewett, was offered the choice between a small theatre, a medium-sized one, and Drury Lane. Unwisely, I fear, he couldn't resist the lure of Drury Lane. Unwisely on two counts: firstly the show was far too small-scale for such a huge theatre, and secondly it would be going in after *My Fair Lady* – to put it mildly, a tough act to follow. *Syracuse* is an adaptation of Shakespeare's *Comedy of Errors*, with two pairs of twins – twin masters and their twin servants. The servants were a young up-and coming Ronnie Corbett and a sweet little Music Hall comedian called Sonny Farrer ('Five feet of Fun and a Banjo') and their masters were Bob Monkhouse and me.

Mr Rodgers himself arrived during rehearsals, and the first words he uttered on seeing Bob and myself were: 'How the hell are we supposed to make you two guys look like twins?' It was a good question. Bob and I were the same age and the same height, but there the resemblance ended. We wore identical costumes, wigs and beards, which helped quite a lot, but there were still one or two problems: I have rather big rugby-player's thighs, and Bob has rather slim elegant comedian's thighs. There was only one way out of this – Bob had to wear padded tights. Also Bob has a nice, civilised, normal nose, whereas mine has what I like to think of as an imposing Roman bridge, which is actually just a bloody great bump, partly inherited, but greatly enhanced by the attentions of that tough kid from

116

Sunderland who gave me such a hard time in the boxing ring at Catterick. There was not much I could do about this, short of major surgery, so once again the adjustment had to be all one way, and poor Bob not only had to pad his tights, but was obliged to stick a not very convincing lump of putty on his nose every night, in a gallant attempt to simulate years of damage with a five-minute nose-job. I don't think he held it against me – we're still good friends.

Although *Syracuse* didn't run *quite* as long as *My Fair Lady*, it was joyous while it lasted, but not so joyous as the arrival of Joanna, daughter number two. Although Stella was now plunged into the classic mother's nightmare of two under two, they were both so beautiful that the joy far outweighed the hassle. Easy for me to say, of course, because I was always gallivanting off to rehearsals every morning or performances every night, and Stella bore the brunt of the work, but she rose to it magnificently, with a little help from several au pair girls of distinctly variable quality.

My old friend Edward Woodward, who once understudied me in the West End back in the '50s, but then went on to do quite nicely for himself, had just spent what he described as 'eighteen months of sheer bloody *purgatory*' on Broadway playing Charles Condamine in *High Spirits*, a musical version of Noël Coward's *Blithe Spirit*. Madam Arcati, the medium, was played by Beatrice Lillie, a great English comedienne renowned for her eccentricity. She never really knew her lines, but the first time Ted tried to help her out of a tight corner, she declaimed in ringing tones, at a live performance in front of a packed paying audience, 'Don't try to prompt *me*, young man!' (He never tried again.) Later in the run she gave an interview with *Time* magazine, and it was arranged that her photograph would be on the front cover. At the last moment, a dodgy military and political situation meant that instead of Bea Lillie, General Westmorland graced the front cover. That evening, during the famous séance scene, Ted had a line something like: 'Are we going back in time, Madam Arcati?'

'Time?' she roared, oblivious to all those people who had paid fifty dollars to see this great scene, '*Time*? Don't talk to me about *Time*! They promised to put my picture on the cover, and now there's this bloody General or Field Marshal or Whatever he's called. *Time*? I'll never buy a copy of it again!'

When the show came to the Savoy in London, I played the part created by Ted, but with dear old reliable Cicely Courtneidge as Madam Arcati. Elvira, my dead first wife (the 'Blithe Spirit' of Noël Coward's title) who materialises after one of Madam Arcati's séances and creates havoc for me and my second wife, was played by a famous actress of great comic talent who had just the right sulky, insinuating personality for Elvira, but whose list of accomplishments did not include looking good on a Kirby wire. In the original play, Elvira simply walks into the room and says, 'Hello, Charles.' This being a musical, something more colourful was called for, and so our Elvira made her first entrance flying on a wire right across the stage and back again before gently coming in to land and then finally (slightly anti-climactically) saying, 'Hello, Charles.'

Flying on a wire is not as easy as it looks, as any actress who has played Peter Pan will tell you, and looking graceful, ghostly, amused, seductive and mischievous all at once, while strapped into a harness and zooming back and forth ten feet above the stage is enough to tax the combined skills of a dancer, actress and circus acrobat, and our lady's early attempts were not a pretty sight, as Noël (who was directing the show himself) made abundantly clear.

'Don't worry, Noël,' said Danny Daniels, the American choreographer. 'I'm gonna work on her – she'll be great.'

A week or so later, he had another go:

'I've been working on her, Noël, and she looks terrific. You wanna have a look?'

'All right,' said Noël grimly. 'Hook her up, hook her up.'

Danny hooked her up and she went through the routine.

'There – how does she look, Noël?'

'She looks like a bag of shit. Cut her down *immediately*.'

A few days later we were working on another scene, and half-way through, having just uttered one of Noël's immortal, beautifully structured lines, she called to him sitting in the stalls, and said:

'Noël, dahling, this line doesn't seem to play awfully well.'

Back from the darkness of the stalls came those perfectly chiselled, slightly effete but implacable tones:

'Perfectly good line, darling, perfectly good line. You might even get a laugh on it if you didn't walk across the stage like a camel with piles while you're saying it.'

That evening, the lyric writer and co-producer Timothy Gray, better known to me as Jack Gray when we were in *Airs on a Shoestring* together, rang me at home and said:

'Oh, Denny, we're letting Elvira go.' That brutal Broadway euphemism for The Sack. So, we let Elvira go, we opened at the Savoy with an American replacement, and the reviews were lukewarm, except for one absolute corker for me from Bernard Levin who said: 'Denis Quilley played Charles Condamine with all the charm and animation of the leg of a billiard table.'

'Oops,' I said to Stella, only half joking, 'this looks like a good time to go to Australia.' So that's what we did.

It so happened that *Robert and Elizabeth*, Ronald Millar's dramat-isation of the romance between Robert Browning and Elizabeth Barrett, with music by Ron Grainer, was all set to go to Melbourne and Sydney. Playing Elizabeth was June Bronhill, Aussie born and bred, all set to make a triumphant return to her home country. She was born in in the opal mining town of Broken Hill (hence the name Bronhill) and had come over to London as a promising young soprano; she joined Sadler's Wells Opera, and quickly rose to become one of their brightest stars. I personally had seen her as a charming, perky Vixen in Janacek's *Cunning Little Vixen*, and a glamorous and ravishingly-sung Merry Widow. When I was asked to play opposite her as Browning, I knew that I was not in her class vocally, but hoped that my acting would make up the deficiency. And so it proved: for a singer she was a very good actress, and for an actor I was a pretty good singer – it made a good combination.

Johnny Ladd, who had been in *Grab Me a Gondola* with me, had gone to Melbourne in 1959 to direct the Australian production, and now lived there permanently, working as the comedy director on Paul Hogan's TV show (some years before Hogan made it big with *Crocodile Dundee*). Johnny wrote offering me a pad in his Melbourne house while we looked for somewhere for the family to live, so I flew out on my own, and Johnny and I went house-hunting in the evenings after my rehearsals. We soon found a charming little house just round the corner from the Melbourne Cricket Ground and a pleasant ten-minute stroll through a small park to the Princess Theatre. While I slogged through the final stages of rehearsals, orchestra calls, technical runs and dress rehearsals, dear sweet generous helpful Johnny sewed curtains and found lampshades and cushions, and generally spruced up the unpretentious little place until it looked like a four-page colour spread in *Australian Woman's Weekly*.

As soon as we opened and it became clear that we were a success and would easily run for the scheduled six months in Melbourne and six more in Sydney, Stella came out with Sarah and Jo, we settled in, and a long love affair with Australia and the Australians began. The Aussies, as we all know, have no time for Whingeing Poms. On the other hand they have a soft spot for a Visiting Star from Overseas, so long as he doesn't put on poncey airs and graces. It doesn't take them long to decide which category to put you in. Fortunately, not being one of nature's whingers, or given to poncey airs and graces, I fitted neatly (if slightly flatteringly) into the Visiting Star From Overseas slot. It also helped that I was obviously experienced and competent at what I did, something that your average Aussie susses very quickly and regards as a prime virtue. In fact, Ian Smith, who played the eldest of the Barrett brothers, suggested that I should give him and some of the boys acting lessons. Maybe a little rubbed off on him – he went on to play Harold in *Neighbours*!

One member of the *Robert and Elizabeth* company who needed no acting lessons from me or anyone else was Frank Thring, who played the tyrannical Papa Barrett, father and absolute ruler of Elizabeth and a whole tribe of boys. You may think you don't know Frank, but you saw him in all those MGM Biblical epics with Charlton Heston, or John Wayne or Kirk Douglas, usually playing a dissolute Herod, sumptuously dressed, hair artfully styled and set, a massive jewelled ring on *every* finger, and a splendid curl to his lip as he spat 'Off with his head' or some equally original and authentically biblical line. As Papa Barrett he was formidable: very camp but with huge authority, using his commanding height and resonant voice to brilliant effect. When he sang 'I'm the master here', by God you believed him.

He could also be very naughty. In one scene I had to burst in energetically into the drawing-room of the Barrett household hoping

121

to find Elizabeth alone and take her away from all this to Italy. I burst energetically, as required – so energetically in fact that as I slammed the door behind me the door-knob came off in my hand. I can see it now – a beautiful Victorian knob of white china with very pretty pink roses on it. I heard the outer knob fall to the floor and, by the sound of it, the spindle with it. There was no way I would be able to get out through that door. Fifteen years had passed since I demolished the back wall of the *Black Arrow* set but nothing had changed – I was as clumsy as ever.

I concealed the knob behind my back in what I hoped was an elegant Victorian gesture, and launched into my impassioned speech to Elizabeth. Halfway through it, as scripted, in came Papa Barrett through the opposite door, from the inner part of the house.

'Mr Browning,' he flung at me with all the force at his command, which was considerable, 'how dare you enter my house without my permission? Leave at once, Sir, and do not presume to return!'

He then turned his back to the audience and, giving me a wicked, gleeful smile, whispered:

'Let's see you get out of this one, dear!'

'Never fear, Mr Barrett,' I replied haughtily and confidently (I'd already got it worked out), 'I am leaving now and you will never see me again.'

I bowed formally and politely to Elizabeth, turned on my heel and strode manfully off the way I had come. I marched resolutely past the useless door until I reached the mercifully large (and mercifully open) sash window which stood next to it, climbed athletically over the window-sill, blew Elizabeth a kiss and dropped gracefully out of sight. The audience applauded as heartily as those undergrads back in Cambridge – nobody seemed to mind that the back-cloth outside the window showed a view of impressive Victorian chimney-pots and the topmost branches of some very tall trees, indicating that we were on an upper floor at least fifty feet above the ground. Perhaps I should have played the next scene on crutches.

Not far from Melbourne, just round the other side of Port Phillip Bay, lies Phillip Island, an unremarkable little piece of land except for one thing – the penguins. Here's what you do: having exhausted the island's charms by taking a gentle afternoon stroll, you arrive at a particular stretch of beach about half an hour before sunset. There you find a sizeable group of people like yourself, plus a tough-looking but gentle and soft-spoken warden, who quietly takes charge from now on. He explains that by some mysterious instinct the penguins know *precisely* when the sun will set. Perhaps they see it, though as they are underwater for the crucial half-hour or so beforehand, this seems unlikely, and even when the sun is obscured by cloud it makes no difference; perhaps they feel a sudden drop in the water temperature, though there is no scientific evidence to support this; the fact remains that somehow or other, they *know*.

Sunset tonight is 7.47, so that is when the action will start. It is now about 7.30, and the warden has switched on some very dim, very unobtrusive lamps which will help you to see clearly without disorienting the penguins; you all sit down on the beach, and he tells you to make sure there is plenty of space between you.

'Right, folks,' he whispers very quietly. 'It's 7.45 now, and the first little fella to arrive will be here in two minutes, at 7.47. So get comfortable, no talking or moving from now on, just keep your eyes open and don't say a word or move a muscle.'

You sit in silence, gazing out at the placid and deserted Tasman Sea; the two minutes pass in still silence, but the expectation and excitement are palpable – you can almost feel each other's hearts beating.

At *exactly* 7.47, a little head pops up from the sea. It looks around, and is delighted to see another little head pop up a few yards away; the two of them swim to meet each other, form up into a pair, swim to the shore, and walk sedately side by side up the beach, past all of you, quietly sitting there, and reach the dunes behind you, where they wait quietly for their friends. Those friends, meanwhile, have all been doing the same, popping up, forming pairs and promenading rather formally up the beach to the dunes: it's rather like the evening passeggiata in the piazza of an Italian town, but sweeter and more childlike because these are so-called fairy penguins, no bigger than a large seagull, and when up on their feet and walking, all but hand in hand, scarcely more than a foot tall.

When they are all met together, there is time for a leisurely chat and a stroll around the dunes to say good evening and introduce their partners to each other, before saying a quiet and polite good night and retiring to bed, each couple to its own little burrow in the sand. It is one of the most moving experiences you will ever have.

An almost equally moving experience is your first sight of Sydney Opera House. Nowadays the whole world is familiar with it – it has become universally admired as the triumphant, defining symbol of the city. In 1969, when I first clapped eyes on it, this was far from the case. There were complaints about how much it was costing and how many much-needed houses could have been built with all that money; serious doubts were expressed about the aesthetic quality of the building and, more seriously, about its structural integrity, all of which, of course, have subsequently been resolved.

When we arrived the outer shell was complete, and work was going ahead on the interior. From the building's inception the plan had always been that the larger of the two main auditoria should house the opera, and the smaller one would be used for orchestral concerts and the like – it was after all the Sydney Opera House, not the Sydney Concert Hall. A pit big enough to hold a full-sized opera orchestra had been built in the larger hall, and vastly expensive stage machinery was already installed, when Mr Davis Hughes, the Minister for the Arts, yielded to pressure from the ABC (the Aussie BBC) and switched horses in mid-stream. The larger auditorium was now to be home for the Sydney Symphony Orchestra, and the opera would be relegated to the smaller hall. The stage machinery was too big to transfer into the smaller space, and was sold off for scrap at an enormous loss; smaller, cheaper and less versatile machinery was installed in the smaller house, and a compromise orchestra pit built.

The end result was an opera house unable to stage international touring productions because of severely restricted wing space, a pit not big enough for a Wagner- or Verdi-sized orchestra, and an auditorium with insufficient seats. At a stroke, Mr Hughes had removed it from the world's grand opera circuit.

Nevertheless, to my eye it was – and still is – one of the most beautiful buildings in the world, as beautiful and uplifting, in its way, as St Paul's Cathedral or the Taj Mahal, and nothing can spoil that thrilling shock of pleasure at seeing it live for the first time: dozens of agile little yachts skimming like dragonflies across the choppy waters of the harbour, the occasional scruffy old motor-boat putt-putting unhurriedly homewards, the ferries chugging importantly out through the Heads to their various destinations up and down this delectable coast, and presiding majestically over it all, its shining white shell glistening in the sunlight, its massive bulk somehow light as air and seeming to defy gravity, stands that fantastical, dreamlike shape – is it a bird, is it a sea-creature, can it be a *building*? – poised and ready at a moment's notice to launch itself into the sea, into the air, into space? It is the perfect gateway into this mercurial city.

I was born in London and lived in it all my life, but I have worked all over the world, and of all the cities I have lived and worked in, Sydney is the one I loved the most and found the hardest to leave. With the energy of Manhattan, the warmth of any Italian city you care to name, a string of fabulous beaches, from Bondi up through Manly and all the way to Whale Beach, and a climate that lets you wear shorts for nine months of the year, the place is irresistible. We didn't even try to resist – we were both instantly seduced.

Our first Sydney home was in Hunter's Hill, a beautiful little enclave of small stone houses designed by French architects and built by Italian stone-masons. A verandah ran across the back of the house with a grapevine entwined around it, and the garden, resplendent with blue-blossomed jacaranda trees, ran right to the edge of the Middle Harbour. This little corner of paradise was an easy drive from the city centre, and very convenient for the theatre while *Robert and Elizabeth* was playing. By the time it ended its six-month run we had both decided that we loved Sydney so much we wanted to stay longer, and two things happened: I was offered the leading role in a TV series for the ABC, which gave us the perfect reason for staying, and Stephen was born. Our beautiful, happy, gentle little son was, in a roundabout way, named after me: I was born in the early hours of Boxing Day, the feast of St Stephen (I almost arrived in the taxi on the way to the hospital but Mum just made it in time) and I was going to be called Stephen in honour of the saint, until she and Dad changed their minds and named me (I like to think) after the French St Denis. So it seemed a nice idea to skip a generation and call our little lad Stephen.

The TV studios were out to the north of the city, so we moved to Palm Beach, about twenty miles up the coast on a peninsula, with

Pittwater, a large inlet very popular for sailing and water-sports, to the West, and the Pacific Ocean to the East. Our house was right at the very tip of the peninsula, looking over a great crescent of beach dominated by the Barrenjoey lighthouse which stood on a narrow strip of sand separating Pittwater and the Ocean. The garden, which sloped in a series of steps down toward the beach, was filled, not with jacarandas this time, but with giant gum-trees, through whose branches flitted dozens of Rosella parrots, pretty colourful little creatures who whistled sweetly – quite unlike the harsh cawing of the big white parakeets which abound in Australia. At dusk the possums visited us on our terrace asking for bananas, which they usually got (*very* hard to say no to these appealing but tenacious little creatures.) We even had a visiting koala bear for a while, dopey on eucalyptus and rolled into a ball, sitting precariously on the branch of a gum-tree near the house.

By now our two girls were at a happy little kindergarten looking over Pittwater, and baby Steve was growing fast. The first season of the TV show had been a great success, and during the break before filming a second series, Darlene Johnson and I were doing a short run of a musical show in the dinner theatre of one of the smarter Sydney hotels. Everything was idyllic, life was beautiful beyond description, and then God hit us with a left and a right.

Australia has its fair share of creepy-crawlies. The red-back and funnel-web spiders are both highly poisonous, there's an octopus that kills you in about two minutes unless you suck or cut the poison out immediately, there are one or two nasty snakes, and lots of mosquitoes. There are irritating but harmless little grass-ticks which get under your skin – we used to spend a few minutes each evening at bed-time picking them out of the girls' bodies, and there are also larger, blood-sucking ticks which can kill a small dog. There was one evening which a paparazzo would have loved to capture, when Stella knelt at my feet using her eye-brow tweezers to pull one of these lethal ticks from the very extremity of a most sensitive part of my anatomy.

But there are also an awful lot of flies. Those pictures of sheep-farmers in the outback wearing big hats with corks dangling from the brim are always good for a laugh, but in truth those tough guys know what they are doing – they are keeping the bloody flies off. Flies are not just a damn nuisance, they carry dirt and they carry diseases, including gastro-enteritis, which is what they gave to little Steve.

Just a bit of a stomach upset, we thought – the local doctors in Palm Beach didn't seem too worried, though they gave us the name of a doctor at the Sydney hospital just in case. Then one day Diana, our au pair girl, who was a trained nurse, said: 'Steve doesn't look too good today – he needs oxygen. I think we should take him to hospital.' She was right – he didn't look good. I rang Dr Simpson at the hospital, he told us to come straight away, and we jumped into the car, leaving Diana with the girls.

It was a Sunday, and the weekend traffic between the city and the beaches was very heavy. I took advantage of every little gap, and floored the accelerator whenever I could. A motor-cycle cop pulled me over for speeding, but Stella cried out, 'My baby is terribly ill!' and he waved us on and escorted us through the traffic for a while, before roaring off.

The first person I saw when we reached the hospital was an efficient looking girl.

'Do you know where Dr Simpson is?'

'Yes.'

'Take me to him.'

She took one look at Steve and ran. We ran after her. Someone took Steve from me and we waited, I don't know how long. Eventually a sweating and distressed young doctor came into the waiting room, took off his surgical mask and said:

'I'm sorry, but by the time we got to him his heart was giving out. We did all we could. I'm afraid we've lost him.'

I can remember turning my face away into the corner of the room, facing the wall like a dunce at school and breathing very deeply to stop from passing out. And a nurse's voice saying, 'Is he all right?' and Stella saying: 'Yes – he's upset, that's all.'

I don't remember driving home, but as we reached the house we both noticed the garbage bins, and simultaneously reminded each other: 'Oh, we must put the dustbins out – the garbos come on Monday morning.' Hanging on to the boring framework of routine somehow stopped us from breaking down. For the same reason, we decided that I should go to work that evening.

I got myself to the dinner theatre, and I got myself through the show. God knows I must have been awful, but I got myself through it. Afterwards, I went to the men's room to clean up, and fell apart. Darlene came in and sat quietly and calmly holding my hand while I cried and cried and cursed God and vilified Australia and cried some more, and when I ran out of tears she drove me home to poor Stella, who was desperately holding on to her sanity while telling the girls we must all try to be happy that Steve had gone to Heaven. My memories of the next few days are perhaps best left undisturbed.

We had had a very brief glimpse of New Zealand for just a few hours while filming a TV episode the previous year, and it seemed a good idea, now that I had a little free time, to take ourselves and the girls over there for a week, both to get away from the scene of our distress, and also to refresh our eyes and our spirits with a slightly cooler atmosphere and landscape after almost three years in Australia. We arranged everything, and on the very day of our departure my sister Paddy telephoned me from London to tell me that Dad had died.

He had been ill for some time, and they had known the end was near. I channelled my grief into anger.

'Why didn't you tell me sooner? Why didn't you let me know what was happening?'

'We didn't want to upset you so soon after losing Steve,' she wept.

'But I could have got there – I could have been with him.'

'In the end it happened quicker than we expected, and then it was too late.'

I raged stupidly on until her husband Mike came onto the line and coolly and gently calmed us both down.

'Don't worry, Den. He wouldn't have known you. He didn't know anyone. It would have been a waste of time and energy to come all that way, and it would only have upset you even more. You carry on with your work – we'll take care of things at this end.'

He was right, of course. His solid, dependable good sense prevailed, and Paddy and I pulled ourselves together, reminisced fondly for a while and said goodbye lovingly.

I sat looking at my family. Our bags were all packed, the car was sitting outside all topped up with petrol, oil and water, tyres at the right pressure, our air tickets were in my pocket, life was still full of good things to see and do. Silly not to go.

Cool, almost frosty mornings, fresh, light green foliage, carefully tended countryside, and sweet, straightforward people: the farmer who, when I called good morning and asked if he know of anywhere we might get lunch, looked at his watch and said, in that lovely twangy drawl, 'Well, you know it's almost twenty-five to two – I don't think you'll find anything anywhere now'; the motorcycle policeman who followed us into the town of Hamilton, pulled me over and said, 'You know how fast you were going?'

'About thirty, I think.' (There was a 30 mph limit.)

'Well, I made it thirty-two. And you could see me right behind you – that looks to me a bit like taking the mickey out of the police.'

'Oh, I certainly didn't intend that, I'm really sorry. It's a hired car – maybe the speedo isn't very accurate?'

By this time he had realised we were well-intentioned, law-abiding Poms, and we had a nice long chat about the weather, the beauties of the countryside, how long we were staying and where we were heading, before he drove off with a wave, crying: 'Have a nice day – and watch that speed!'

The hot springs at Rotorua, a row-boat on Lake Taumarunui, one way and another the week flew by, the girls enjoyed it as much as we did, and we got back to Sydney with our hearts lighter than when we left.

We were still in love with Australia, and began thinking very seriously about staying in Sydney permanently, or at least on a long-term basis. We loved the way of life, we loved the people, but after staying up all night talking it through we realised that from the professional point of view it was a dead end. At this time (the late '60s) there was virtually no seriously professional theatre apart from touring productions of London and New York successes – mostly musicals and light comedies – and the film and TV industries had not begun to get off the ground in the way they have today.

'Where is the challenge?' said Stella. 'Where are Laurence Olivier, John Gielgud, the National Theatre, the Royal Shakespeare Company?,' words which were, as we shall see, totally prophetic. There was, in the end, no argument. We had to go home.

Chapter 8
The Impossible Dream

AS THE TAXI from Victoria Station chugged through the drizzle up the hill to Hampstead we looked at each other in dismay: could this really be the beautiful place we knew and loved so well?

Perhaps the almost unbearable misery of losing our son and my father in such brutally quick succession had embittered us and darkened our vision of the world about us, but, whatever the reason, London seemed very grey and uninviting after so long away. After the vast spaces and positive, free-and-easy attitudes we had enjoyed for almost three years, everything felt cramped, drab and cautious. The buildings hemmed us in, diminishing the sky, and instead of, 'No worries sport, she'll be right' it was, 'No we don't stock that, we find there's no call for it.'

Gradually, of course, things fell back into place as familiar routines took over. Our local shopkeepers and old Maggie the flower-seller on the corner were pleased to see us back, our eyes adjusted to the softer light and the smaller but greener English landscape, and Hampstead Heath, that miraculously preserved breathing-space on our doorstep, was as glorious as ever. The girls went to the Church of England primary school just up the road, and life started settling into a new and comfortable groove.

But first, Mum had to be looked after. Steve's death had deeply upset her, but losing Dad had shattered her. She and Cliff had known each other all their adult lives; he was the only man in her life, ever; he was her rock, her comforter, her mentor, and without him she was bewildered and confused, like a lost child. She was also physically unwell, and was in hospital when we arrived home. She could not bear to return to the empty house where she and Cliff had spent all those years together, and we had to sort out where she would live. Paddy and Mike's house was too small for her to share, but we had two spare rooms, and so long as she could get up the stairs it would suit her very well – she would have her own kitchen and bathroom and be completely independent, but within call for any emergency.

When I visited her in hospital, the Ward Sister said, with a sceptically raised eyebrow,

'I gather you haven't room for your mother to live with you – is that right?'

I looked at Mum, who looked sheepishly away. I knew exactly what she had said to the Sister: 'Oh no, they won't want me there, they've got young children, they don't want an old woman getting under their feet and being in the way. Anyway, they haven't got room.' She loathed the idea of being a burden and a nuisance – I understood of course, I would have felt the same.

'Don't worry,' I said to the Sister. 'We'll sort it out.'

Everything was arranged: after her discharge from hospital, she was going to a convalescent home for two weeks, which would give us time to organise her living arrangements. With help from the Sister we chose a convalescent home in Frinton-on-Sea, in Essex. It was a sentimental and nostalgic choice: all our family holidays when I was a little boy had been in Clacton, just along the coast from Frinton. Well, not quite in Clacton, to be precise: we had a beach hut in Little Holland, and we went there year after year. Little Holland was, we liked to think, a little more genteel than Clacton proper, but the real toffs, of course, went to Frinton. So Mum was returning to her old haunts in some style.

I picked her up from the hospital and drove her down to Frinton. She was a little uncomfortable on the journey, but quite chirpy, and eager to point out familiar landmarks as we reached the seaside. We found the convalescent home, which was attractive and beautifully situated, a nun welcomed us and showed us to a pleasant little room, got Mum into her night clothes and into bed, and left us to get settled in and have a chat before I left. We talked of this and that, and how I would pop down in a few days and then come and fetch her when the two weeks were up. Then she said, quite calmly and unemotionally: 'I want to die, Den.'

I was so shocked and upset that I said all the wrong things – what about Paddy and me, what about her grandchildren – all the predictable, selfish reactions, and the more upset I got, the louder I got, bringing a worried nun bustling in to see what was going on. I reassured her and calmed down, and Mum and I had a nice quiet chat, and I took my leave, promising to come down and see her at the weekend.

She died that night.

Why did I not understand? Why did I get so angry and upset? Of course she wanted to join Cliff – wherever he had gone, that was where she wanted to be. And there they are now, happily dancing to Lehar's 'Gold and Silver' waltz.

Once again the cure for the pain was to plunge into hard work and the exacting timetable of rehearsals and opening nights; to shake the brain out of its torpor, stop it from wallowing in regrets and self-reproach, and make it focus on the future. This determination to pick myself up and start afresh was made easier by two very different events: our son David arrived, filling the black void in our lives with sunshine and laughter, and I acquired a new agent. There is nothing, absolutely nothing, so excruciatingly boring as listening to an actor talking about his agent, so here are a few words about my agent.

Bernard Hunter started his career at seventeen singing with Henry Hall and the BBC Dance Orchestra. He couldn't play an instrument, so when he sat in with the band he strummed a guitar with rubber strings, which made him look very dashing and grown-up, and fortunately made no sounds loud enough for the BBC microphones to pick up. He went on to become an accomplished performer in the theatre, appearing with the likes of Dickie Henderson and the great Syd Field, and married Eve Lister, one of the most beautiful and talented musical comedy stars of her day.

I first met him in 1953, when we worked together in the revue at the Royal Court which I mentioned earlier, *Airs on a Shoestring*. Some years after that he gave up performing and formed an agency with his partner Terry Owen. My return from Australia in 1969, and my need for a fresh start, prompted me to accept his long-standing offer to join him, and we have been together ever since. Friends for forty-five years and professional partners for thirty years – is this some kind of record? And there's life in both the old dogs yet.

I told myself that I must make this year a turning point – I must start doing some Serious Theatre before it was too late. I had turned forty, my days as a romantic leading man in musicals were surely numbered, and I needed – and wanted – to summon up my courage and stand toe-to-toe with the big men – Shakespeare, Chekhov, O'Neill, and any other heavyweights who would do me the honour of accepting my challenge. Fortunately, right on cue, up came an offer I couldn't refuse – to play Archie Rice in John Osborne's wonderful study of a third-rate music hall comedian, *The Entertainer*, at the new Nottingham Playhouse, a splendid auditorium and a very far cry from the dear little old Nottingham Rep where Stella and I had thrilled the patrons with our Dandini and Demon King fifteen years before. *The Entertainer* went splendidly, and I stayed on to play Macbeth, a much tougher examination which I think I passed, if not with first class honours, at least with credit.

Back in London, I told Bernard that this was definitely the way I wanted to go, and that I would really like to join one of the two major companies, the Royal Shakespeare Company, or the National Theatre, and preferably the National, which at this time was based at the Old Vic Theatre and led by Laurence Olivier, who had been my idol and my inspiration since I was a schoolboy.

'I would give my eye-teeth to work with Olivier,' I said.

'Who wouldn't?' laughed Bernard. 'Let's see what we can do.'

Two days later he rang me.

'You won't believe this, but Olivier wants to see you about joining the National for the next season.'

I was stunned with amazement and delight – 'What did you do?'

'Nothing – they called out of the blue.'

In fact, I learned later that Olivier and director Michael Blakemore had been in Nottingham discussing a projected National Theatre tour, and had been to see me as Archie Rice and Macbeth – two roles with which Olivier was rather familiar. Thank God I didn't know he was watching!

Now I knew that the National were planning to stage *Guys and Dolls* that season, with Olivier playing Nathan Detroit, so it was obvious that they wanted to take on someone who had a lot of experience in musicals. But I also knew that they were doing Shakespeare's *Coriolanus* with Christopher Plummer in the title role. There are some parts that you just know you can play, and there was a part in *Coriolanus* which I knew I could play with one hand tied behind my back – Aufidius, Coriolanus's great antagonist. But there was, of course, no chance that they would offer such a crucial role to a newcomer in the company, especially one whose major leading roles in the West End had all been in musicals. Never mind – doing *Guys and Dolls* would be a way of getting into the company, and if, with a bit of luck, other weightier roles should come up, then I would be really able to show them what I could do.

The offices of the National Theatre of Great Britain and Northern Ireland were down the road from the Old Vic in a higgledy-piggledy assemblage of rather sweet little wooden shacks overshadowed by large blocks of council flats in Aquinas Street, a nondescript thoroughfare named, presumably, after St Thomas of that ilk, a man famous for his ability to dictate to four secretaries at once – a gift which would have been a great asset to the devoted little band of people who worked unstintingly to keep this cultural outpost up and running.

At the appointed time I entered one of these little shacks to be confronted by a formidable triumvirate – John Dexter, Michael Blakemore and the Boss, the Guvnor, your actual Laurence Olivier. He was unbuttoned, both literally (jacket over a chair, waistcoat undone, tie loosened and shirt open at the neck) and metaphorically – a big guffaw that would have been heard at the Festival Hall, in response, I imagine, to a typically elegant and barbed witticism from Dexter. I just hoped it wasn't about me.

'Ah, Mr Quilley,' he said, still laughing. 'Welcome. Sit down. We've asked you here because we'd like you to join our little company.'

Our little company? Some of the greatest actors in the country, led by the greatest of them all? Join our *little company*? What do you say? (I think I probably said thank you.)

'And the first part we'd like you to play would be Aufidius in *Coriolanus*.'

Somehow I managed not to jump up and turn cartwheels all around the shack – well, there wasn't room, anyway. But Catherine wheels and Roman candles definitely went off in my head. As I got up to leave, he said:

'Oh – you sing a bit too, don't you? We must try to fit you into *Guys and Dolls* as well.'

Manfred Weckwerth and Joachim Tenschert were directors of the renowned Berliner Ensemble, and a few years previously they had staged a legendary production of Brecht's *Coriolan*, a play which is based on the same episode of Roman history as Shakespeare's *Coriolanus* but is, of course, an entirely new and very different piece. The National Theatre's Literary Manager (he preferred the more exotic and cosmopolitan title of Dramaturg) was Kenneth Tynan, a formidable, sometimes cruel, critic, but a passionate lover of the theatre. Ken had had the brilliant idea of inviting the two Germans to come to London and direct a production of Shakespeare's *Coriolanus*. The possibilities of completely fresh insights into this great text were enormous, and Olivier was won over to the idea. An emissary was duly dispatched to Berlin to present the idea to the two men, who accepted with alacrity and great enthusiasm.

So here we all are in the rehearsal room up under the roof of the Old Vic: Christopher Plummer, Constance Cummings, Charles Kay, Anna Carteret, John Moffat, Bernard Gallagher, Michael Turner and me, very keyed up and excited and straining at the leash to make my National Theatre debut. In come Weckwerth and Tenschert, looking twitchy, and in strolls Olivier, with that shoulder-swinging gait of his, looking gloomy.

'Bit of a cock-up, chaps,' he says, eyeballs rolling heavenwards just as they did in *Lady Hamilton* when Horatio Nelson said with a wry smile, 'For God's sake get me a doctor,' before collapsing in agony on the floor. 'Let's just read through the Shakespeare so that the boys can hear all your voices, then we'll have a bit of a chat.'

Read through the Shakespeare? What else would we read through – it's all we've got in front of us. We read through the Shakespeare. (Quite well, actually, considering the peculiar circumstances.) Then we have lunch and reconvene, and discover what this is all about. It transpires that while the National Theatre is adamant that 'The Boys' were invited to direct Shakespeare's *Coriolanus*, the Boys themselves are swearing blind that they were asked to direct an English translation of Brecht's *Coriolan*. A bit of a cock-up indeed.

There's something of a stalemate for a while. Or perhaps I mean a stand-off. Perhaps I even mean a Mexican stand-off? Eventually a compromise is reached: the Boys will direct Shakespeare's play, but they will 'adapt' it first, if we don't mind. So we spend the first week rehearsing in piecemeal fashion while the script is cut, rearranged and reshaped, to get it into a Brechtian form. Now the typical Brechtian form is a series of shortish scenes, each of which is brought to an end by a traverse curtain sliding across to stop the action and to enable a few lines of information to be projected onto a screen above it, telling you what is going to happen next. This is part of Brecht's famous (notorious?) Alienation Effect, and it means, of course, among other things, that the action is stopped and re-started a dozen or more times during the course of the evening, whereas Shakespeare, as we know, wrote for an open stage on which as one group of actors were finishing a scene and going off, the next group would overlap and come on to start the following scene, allowing the action to proceed in one continuous flow.

Besides putting the play into Brechtian form, the other reason for this reshaping of the text was to try to make it convey a Brechtian message, and Brecht's message, of course is a strongly and didactically socialist one. *Coriolanus* is assuredly a political play, inasmuch as it is a play about politics, but Shakespeare's concern, as always, is to show the emotional effect that these political events have upon his characters, whereas Brecht's concern, on the contrary, is to use the characters to make his own political statement.

For example, there is a wonderful scene in which Coriolanus's mother Volumnia (memorably played by Edith Evans when Olivier himself played Coriolanus in 1959) kneels before her son and begs him not to march against his own people in Rome; this somehow became a scene in which Coriolanus hears the citizens arming, and decides that he cannot march against 'The workers'. When Olivier saw this scene in rehearsal, he said, 'Funny – I always thought it was something to do with his mother.' Chris Plummer saw the writing on the wall (and also saw that the design for his costume was a little unflattering), and promptly pulled out and hot-footed it back to Hollywood. Anthony Hopkins was instantly drafted in to replace him, and we all worked with a will to try to bring this strange hybrid creature to life.

We brought it off rather better than one might have expected. The Boys, despite their daft conviction that they could turn Shakespeare into something he wasn't, were canny and experienced theatre men, and the production had some fine moments, though it also had many moments when I, for one, was waiting in the wings with every nerve in my body urging me to go on and pick up where Tony Hopkins was leaving off, only to have to wait while that bloody curtain came across and announced: 'Aufidius returns and finds that the town has been taken' and then have to go on and say: 'The town is taken.'

The critical reaction was, as we in the trade delicately say, mixed, though I personally came out of it unscathed and was, of course, selfishly delighted that my debut had been successful. Now, I thought, if only I can be in a play with the man himself, actually tread these historic boards side by side with the Guvnor, I'll be able to tell my grandchildren and die happy. When he asked me to play his son Jamie in the next production, Eugene O'Neill's gut-wrenching four-and-a-half-hour masterpiece *Long Day's Journey into Night*, I could hardly contain my joy.

I mentioned earlier that the two plays which have always stayed with me from this wonderful period were the two American ones. *Long Day's Journey* was one, of course, and the other was *The Front Page*.

Hecht and MacArthur's deeply cynical but irresistibly funny script features a group of unscrupulous, unsentimental newspaper reporters sitting around in the Press Room of a Chicago prison waiting impatiently for an imminent hanging to take place in time for them to phone the story to their editors. It was given an electrifying production by Michael Blakemore. Halfway through the play the condemned man escapes from his cell and, to quote the stage direction, 'climbs in through the open window of the Press Room'. This was not dramatic enough for Blakemore. He ordered his designer to produce an enormous window made of sugar-glass, which looked exactly like plate-glass, and instead of climbing in, Clive Merrison, who played the prisoner, swung on a rope like Tarzan, crashed spectacularly through the window, and landed flat on his face on the floor, producing wild laughter and applause from the audience, and terrified screams from the ladies in the front row, onto whose laps the harmless but alarmingly realistic shards of glass showered every night. And every night another new, expensive window had to be installed, only to be shattered in its turn. A stage manager's nightmare.

Long Day's Journey inhabits another world; still unmistakably and quintessentially American, but a world peopled by past regrets and present sorrows, wasted talents and broken dreams, fears for the future and fierce love–hate family relationships – a thinly-disguised portrait of O'Neill's own family. I find it fascinating that he resorted to the use of Greek masks (in *The Great God Brown*) and classical mythology (in *Mourning becomes Electra*) in a desperate search for universality in his themes, and finally achieved a masterpiece of undisputed universal significance by going back to his roots and writing about his own family.

I have always been firmly convinced that in the performing arts, shorter is virtually always better. There are very, very few dramatic works which earn an audience's attention for much longer than two and a half or, at a pinch, three hours. Some of Wagner's operas, I suppose, although even there I would happily lose an hour or so. But *Long Day's Journey* justifies every minute of its four and a half hours. We ran the first three acts straight through for the first half of the evening, which meant that the only interval came after about two and a half hours, then the last act ran for something over an hour and a half. The packed audiences were rapt and silent from beginning to end: never did it seem to them or to us a moment too long.

For the first week or two of rehearsals I was hardly able to concentrate on my own character, so consumed was I by the excitement of working with Olivier. At one point the director, Michael Blakemore, suggested a change of move, and I replied:

'But if I move there I'm worried about getting in Sir Laurence's way.'

'Oh, my darling boy,' cried Olivier, grasping me by the shoulders and beaming into my face, 'you really must call me Larry.'

I paused, gritted my teeth, grinned sheepishly and said, 'I'll try, I'll try.' I managed it, of course, and we became good friends, so henceforth in these pages Larry is what I shall call him.

On another day we were rehearsing a scene in which he and I had to catch each other's eye behind Connie Cummings' back when we suspect she is on the dope again.

'Are you looking at me, dear boy?'

'Yes, Larry, I am.'

'Are you sure, because I can't see your eyes without my glasses.'

'I promise you, I'm looking you right in the eye.'

'Oh good, good. I used to have the opposite problem, you know – my eyesight was so sharp that I had to de-focus my eyes when I was playing out front because I hated being able to see the audience's faces.'

I had to laugh. I knew him well enough now to be able to say: 'Come on – what about that opening soliloquy of *Richard III*? You came on through that door in the upstage left corner, did a double take on the audience, limped slowly all the way down the centre of the footlights, and then took about five minutes to count the house before launching into "Now is the winter of our discontent".'

'Oh, darling boy,' he replied, 'I would never do anything so vulgar as to count the house. In any case, in that production there was no need to – it was full at every performance.'

Watching him work was like watching a terrier hunting a rat. He would spend hours nagging away at tiny pieces of business – lighting a cigar, opening his pocket-watch, lifting a drink – until they were second nature to the character and completely integrated into the whole. He would make an entrance, go off, enter again, go off again and enter yet again until he was satisfied that he was bringing on the right emotional mood, the right tone of voice and the right body language. He grabbed O'Neill's script and never let go until he had beaten it into submission, and then he cherished it and loved it like a horse he had broken, which would now happily work with him and carry him wherever he wanted to go.

As we neared the end of rehearsals I said to Ronald Pickup, who was playing my brother: 'You know what? I think this is going to be one of those landmark productions – I think that when we are old and grey we are going to tell people, "I was in that!"'

And so it proved. The opening night was a triumph. Larry and I held hands at the curtain call, and as we bowed in response to the tumultuous cheers he whispered: 'We're very, very lucky.'

My impossible dream had come true.

I took Stella to his room after the curtain finally came down. I knocked on his door. 'Who is it?' came the rather wheezy cry. 'It's Stella.' 'Bring her in, darling, bring her in.'

In we went, and there he was, sprawled back in his armchair wearing nothing but his underpants and a tired but happy smile.

'Stella, baby, how lovely to see you – thank you for coming. Forgive me if I don't get up – I've just done fifteen rounds with Muhammad Ali.'

The critics next day were unanimous, and we had a sell-out run at the Albery Theatre before returning to our real home at the Old Vic.

The physical burden on Larry was enormous – he was in his office in Aquinas Street every day running the day-to-day affairs of the National Theatre, and coming to the theatre to play this huge and enormously demanding role every night. On Saturdays a 1 o'clock matinée ended at about 5.30, then the 6.30 evening performance ended just before 11pm. He was 65 at the time, and had quite recently survived cancer and a thrombosis, and was carrying a work-load that would have daunted a fit man half his age.

After the first scene of the play, we took a two-minute pause to let latecomers in, and there was a chair in the wings for Larry to sit on while we waited. On many evenings he would sink exhausted onto the chair and fall instantly asleep. I would give him about a minute and a half and then jog his shoulder gently and say, 'Guv – we're on.' 'Oh, Christ – which scene?' 'After lunch.' 'Right. After lunch. After lunch. Right.' Stand up, clear the throat, square the shoulders and on. On one night only did his fatigue get the better of him, and even then the audience never knew. In the last act he had a long scene with Ron Pickup, in which he drunkenly bemoaned the fact that he could have been a great Shakespearean actor if he hadn't wasted years touring in *The Count of Monte Cristo*, and told a long and rambling story of how he and the great Booth had played *Othello* together, alternating the roles of Othello and Iago, ending with Booth telling the theatre manager, 'That young man is playing Othello better than I ever did.' On this one tired night, he couldn't remember Booth's name, he couldn't remember which play they acted in, and after ad-libbing quite ingeniously for a minute or two, with a little help from Ron, he got up from the table saying, 'I'm sorry lad, you'll have to excuse me, I'm not feeling too well' and staggered off the stage. Ron could do nothing except sit there, take another drink of cold tea masquerading as whisky, and try to look relaxed while thinking to himself (as he confessed to me later): 'I'm on stage the night the Boss drops off the twig! I'm going to be in all the history books for all the wrong reasons!!'

Meanwhile, as Larry lurched into the wings, the stage manager leapt to his feet saying, 'Are you all right, Sir Laurence – can I get you a brandy or something?'

'Never mind the brandy – what's the bloody line?' said Larry, thumbing through the prompt script. 'Ah, yes – Booth and Othello.' Plunge back on stage – 'Sorry about that, lad – where was I? Ah, yes – Booth and my Othello' and on went the scene. Nobody suspected a thing.

I loved him – as the discerning reader may well have guessed by now. Not everybody did; everybody admired him and respected him, of course, for all the obvious reasons, but I loved him – for reasons perhaps a little less obvious. Although a natural-born scene-stealer, he was a generous colleague on stage, always giving you space and time for your important moments, never upstaging you or trying to attract attention to himself when it should be on you. He was also completely devoid of starry pretensions – prima-donna tantrums were not on his agenda. When we filmed the TV version of *Long Day's Journey*, we were booked into Lew Grade's ATV Studios for four days and stayed there for ten, non-stop. The director, Peter Wood, was a perfectionist, and since the film was pre-sold to the USA, he was quite unmoved by Lew Grade's hand-wringing laments about the expense of all that extra studio time and the disruption of other programmes. We were playing in the theatre several evenings as well, so this was, to put it mildly, a heavy schedule. By the end of the first week we were all feeling the strain, and the demands for extra takes of so many scenes were becoming increasingly irksome, but Larry never complained. On about day nine, the lighting-cameraman whispered to me: 'Doesn't he ever blow his top?' He was so accustomed to so-called stars behaving like martinets and bullying their dressers and make-up girls, that he was astonished at the way in which the most powerful and revered man in his profession simply got his head down and did his work. Whenever aspiring young actors ask me (as, touchingly, they quite often do) what is the secret of success in the theatre, I think of Larry and say, 'Hard graft.'

But what I loved most of all about him was the broad streak of vulgarity that lived quite comfortably alongside the sweetness, the toughness and the commanding authority of his nature. I mean this as a great compliment: he was vulgar in the sense that a great comedian like Frankie Howerd was vulgar – he was in touch with the common man. (My old school Latin dictionary says 'Vulgus – the common people.') It was a quality which enabled him to play

146

Archie Rice so poignantly, or to play Richard III with such outrageous, crowd-pleasing chutzpah. The other theatrical knights of his generation (Gielgud, Guinness, Richardson, Redgrave) were all, for want of a more elegant word, gents. Larry never quite was – he was always one of us.

This endearing quality showed itself, just now and then, in his clothes. He had some beautiful suits, and he also had some very jolly ones. My particular favourite was the one I privately christened the Brighton Bookie suit (he was living in Brighton at the time). It was a gloriously robust mustard colour, with a bold brown over-check, matching waistcoat – the business. Then there was the Syd Field overcoat, an ankle-length camel-hair number with very broad shoulders which made him look absolutely square – Mr Five by Five. (Although he could give the impression of commanding height on stage, he actually stood eye-to-eye with me at about five feet ten.) And for a brief period he sported a Sherlock Holmes deerstalker – one of those tweed hats with a peak fore and aft and ear pieces which tie over the top. I think someone must have given him this one for Christmas – it didn't stay on display for very long. But there arrived a day when it came magnificently into its own. He was, as I say, living in Brighton at this time, and his preferred mode of transport was a London black taxi which he had bought and had resprayed in the imperial Olivier purple. The interior also was upholstered in purple, and there was a magnificent stereo system to play his favourite tapes of Beethoven and Wagner and so on. On this wondrous day, we had just done a performance of Long Day's Journey; his chauffeur was off-duty and he was driving himself down to Brighton. As I came out of the stage door after the show, I was stopped in my tracks by a beatific vision. The purple taxi was throbbing at the kerbside, and at the wheel sat the Baron Olivier wearing all three of the above-mentioned items all together at one and the same time in one heart-stopping ensemble: the Brighton Bookie Suit, the Syd Field Overcoat, and in its rightful place as crowning glory, the Sherlock Holmes deerstalker. And booming out of the hi-fi, I promise you, came 'The Ride of the Valkyrie'! I leaned back weakly against the Stage Door, and, unable to stop myself, burst out laughing. He leaned across to the nearside window, fixing me with those hooded grey eyes which Peter O'Toole used to say could turn a man to stone at twenty paces, then, his lips twitching with the merest trace of a smile, he raised two fingers at me in a time-honoured salute, growled: 'Piss off, Quilley!' and roared off down the Waterloo Road towards the Elephant and Castle and the Old Kent Road.

We were a small and tightly-knit company at the Old Vic. Larry had surrounded himself with a group of actors he liked, and whose work he admired; we all – actors, stage managers, technicians and management – knew each other and got on well; we only had one auditorium to fill, so there was great unity of purpose, and the repertoire system meant that the work was constantly varied and stimulating. To play, as I did, Macbeth, Lopakhin in *The Cherry Orchard* and Hildy Johnson in *The Front Page* all in one season, in the company of people like Diana Rigg, Michael Hordern and Constance Cummings, is surely the theatre actor's dream scenario. It was twelve hours a day, six days a week for much of the time, and we were often tired – but never bored. This kind of repertoire programme has its pitfalls, of course, as well as its joys. With three, four or even five productions playing in rotation in one season, each time a play comes back after a break it is almost like a first night. We always tried to have a run-through or at least a sit-down rehearsal on these occasions, but of course other productions were usually being rehearsed during the day, and it was often difficult to get everyone together.

On one such occasion *Richard II*, in which I played Bolingbroke, had been out of the repertoire for about three and a half weeks – an exceptionally long period. For various logistical reasons it proved impossible to rehearse, and we went on cold. In the first scene, there is a crucial moment when Bolingbroke, the King's great adversary, throws down a gauntlet as a challenge to the Duke of Mowbray, saying: 'Pale, trembling coward, now I throw my gage!' Mowbray replies, 'And now I pick it up' – battle is joined and the play is launched on its course. In the hassle and rush to get the production back on, I had not made my pre-show checks with my usual care, and as I approached the crucial moment I put my hand to my belt to check that the gauntlet glove was tucked in there as usual, to discover – no glove. I fought down my panic, my brain went into overdrive, and instead of 'Pale trembling coward, now I throw my gage,' I turned to the assembled full company and cried: 'Who hath a glove? Hath any man a glove?' Now that is actually quite a creditable iambic pentameter, considering the speed with which it was composed. Unfortunately no man had a glove. There were helmets and tabards by the dozen, chain mail by the yard, but not a glove to be seen. All I succeeded in doing was to reduce twenty-five grown men to tears of helpless laughter. The set for this production was a huge raised platform in the shape of England, and Ben Whitrow, who was playing the Bishop of Somewhere-or-other and was standing in Norfolk, round about Great Yarmouth, laughed so much that he fell off into the Wash. Meanwhile, Mowbray was looking at me with an expression which said: 'Come on – we're not off the hook yet.' By this time, however, my powers of invention were exhausted, and all I could come up with was, 'Pale trembling coward, now *would* I throw my gage.' After another look which clearly implied, 'Is that the best you can do?' Mowbray said, 'Now *would* I pick it up!' and on we went, relieved but less than triumphant.

Halfway through rehearsals for *Macbeth* I got my first glimpse of the simple sweetness and charm which were such a surprisingly large ingredient in Olivier's complex personality. My son David had come to Aquinas Street (where there was a large rehearsal room as well as the aforementioned offices) to watch me rehearse a sword-fight with Anthony Hopkins. After the rehearsal I was carrying him on my shoulders to the car park, and as we walked past Olivier's office the window opened and he stuck his head out saying,

'Hallo – would you like some of my lunch?' and offered David a slice of apple, which was gratefully accepted.

'Who are you then?' asks the Guvnor.

'I'm David and I'm four,' says Dave, rather aggressively.

'Four! What a marvellous age to be – I can remember when I was four, thinking to myself: "Thank God I'm not three any more!"'

Dave feels ten feet tall.

Shortly after *Macbeth* opened, however, I was treated at close quarters to a display of another aspect of Larry's protean personality – his monumental and awe-inspiring anger.

Anthony Hopkins was playing Macbeth, Diana Rigg was Lady Macbeth, and I was playing Banquo. Tony is a wonderful actor, who has found his true métier as a film star – he enjoys film acting and he is very, very good at it. Sometimes he was equally good in the theatre – sometimes, but not always. By his own admission he lacked the mental and emotional stamina which is needed when you have to screw yourself up to concert pitch every night and give of your very best eight times a week to a discerning, live audience, especially if you have been rehearsing another play during the day. It is, contrary to the popular conception of an actor's life, *extremely* hard work, and Tony was by no means alone in sometimes seeing it as a life of unrewarding drudgery. On top of this, of course, was his well documented and freely admitted over-reliance on the booze to keep him going.

During early rehearsals his Macbeth seemed to be developing well, but at some point he lost it, and on the opening night he was not good. He knew he was not good, and most of the critics the next day agreed with him. On the second night I waited in the wings for him to join me for our first entrance together, and as he arrived, floating gaily on a bottle or so of vodka, he boomed loudly in that stirring Welsh baritone: 'I wish I was a thousand bloody miles away from here, boyo!'

'Hallo,' I thought to myself. 'We're in for a rough evening.' And we were, rather.

The stage manager's nightly report revealed that the performance lasted twenty-five minutes longer than usual, and during that time we were at the receiving end of an extraordinary feast of quite incompatible ingredients: endless pauses while searches for once-familiar lines were carried out somewhere in the subconscious; long passages of improvisation (some meaningful, some not) when those searches turned up nothing of value; many flashes of blazing brilliance which made your hair stand on end when the right emotion and the right line came briefly together and lit up the stage with something like genius; and long stretches of the bored, colourless delivery of someone just going through the motions.

This went on for about a week or so of wildly different performances, some fast, some slow, some good, some terrible, some audible, some not, with the great Diana Rigg somehow managing to hold it all together by sheer willpower and force of personality; and then one Tuesday morning Larry came up to the rehearsal room where we were working on *The Cherry Orchard*, and beckoned me across to him.

'Darling boy, can you play Mackers on Friday?'

'No. Why – what's happened?'

'Tony's fucked off.'

'Ah. I see. Well, I'm sure you've spoken to him, but would it help if I rang him and asked if he can hang on until I'm ready?'

He went purple. I thought he was going to have a stroke or a heart attack and die before my eyes. Then the voice burst out with all the force of the entire brass section of the London Symphony Orchestra:

'Don't go *near* the fucking phone! I never want to see the little bastard in this building EVER AGAIN!'

'All right, Guvnor, I'll do it –'

'Ungrateful little sod. Brought him up from nothing and gave him –'

'Guv – it's all right. I can do it.'

'I could murder him with my bare –'

'Larry, please, don't worry – it's all right.'

I had to sit him down and repeatedly reassure him that I could do it in the time – four days – before it returned to the repertoire. I had played it before, after all, though some years ago in Rep and in an entirely different production. The lines would come back – it would be all right. He finally calmed down and left the room, still quivering with suppressed rage. The assembled company breathed a unanimous and simultaneous sigh of relief, wished me the best of luck, and turned their attention back to the gentle ironies of Anton Chekhov, while I staggered off to find my battered script of *Macbeth*.

In the event all was well. I surprised everybody – even myself. I managed to get one afternoon's rehearsal with Diana Rigg, who was, of course, wonderfully helpful and supportive, and cheered me up enormously at one point halfway through the afternoon. We had reached the scene in which the idea of murdering Banquo is first openly hinted at. The thought arouses them sexually, and the end of the scene suggests that they go off to bed together. Tony had come up with the rather good idea of caressing Diana's bosom during the last few lines, but unfortunately he did it on the outside of her dress, which had a typically Elizabethan bodice, and was about as sexy as caressing a plank of wood.

'What I really ought to do,' I started to say, 'is –'

'Of course, baby,' she grinned, anticipating my ploy. 'Go down *inside* the dress.'

I needed no further encouragement, and as my hand comfortably reached the inviting target, I intoned the Thane's great words:

'Light thickens, and the crow makes wing to the rooky wood –' while Diana's famously beautiful Emma Peel voice whispered in my ear –

'Up a bit – left a bit – golden shot!'

Michael Blakemore was baffled that we finished the scene shaking with laughter, but I think Shakespeare would have loved it.

The last play to be staged at the Old Vic before we moved to Denys Lasdun's monumental concrete pile on the South Bank was Peter Hall's production of *The Tempest*, in which I renewed my acquaintance with John Gielgud after a gap of twenty-five years. He was playing Prospero for the third time in his career, and I was Caliban. John was by now over seventy, but the years had not diminished his mastery of the art of verse speaking – if anything it seemed more natural, unforced and effortless than ever. Effortless, however, was not the word to describe our dress rehearsal. John Bury had designed an exotic set dominated by a great golden sun which took the whole evening to travel with majestic slowness from East to West. There were two great black rocks which slid across the stage on tracks to form Prospero's cell and Caliban's cave (which I in my bare feet had to avoid like the plague in case they amputated my toes) and there were trapdoors for eye-catching entrances and exits.

Somewhere round about midnight, after many hours of unremitting toil, John was launching into the great speech in the last act in which he reveals his identity to the lords who have landed on his island:

> ... know for certain
> That I am Prospero, and that very duke
> Which was thrust forth of Milan, who most strangely
> Upon this shore where you were wrecked, was landed
> To be the lord on't – A-a-ah!

and he disappeared from view, dropping like a stone through a trapdoor. There was total silence, no-one spoke, no-one breathed, and then Peter Hall, never previously known for his athletic prowess, *ran* from the production desk at the back of the stalls down to the edge of the stage and, in a voice of preternatural calm which barely concealed the panic and incipient hysteria bubbling beneath the surface, breathed: 'John? Are you all right?' After an agonising pause, those uniquely velvety, fluting tones wafted elegantly up through the gaping hole in the stage, saying, 'Yes, I *think* I'm all right. Can someone get me back up again?' Fortunately for John, though less fortunately for the young man concerned, he had landed on top of the actor playing Ferdinand, who was waiting to come up through the trap for his chess game with Miranda. We carried on.

Half an hour later, one of the big black rocks trundled across the stage, hit John smack in the face and knocked him flat on the floor. This is it, I thought – he'll burst into tears and say, 'For God's sake, somebody take me home, I can't stand any more.' He picked himself up, dusted himself down, and said, 'I think we should call this the *Rocky Horror Show*, don't you?' and soldiered on to the end. I should have known that in his own willowy, diffident fashion, he was just as tough and workmanlike as Larry.

The opening night went wonderfully well until the moment when I had to perform one of the most beautiful speeches in the play which Shakespeare, with exquisitely touching irony, puts into the mouth of the misshapen, half-human Caliban:

> Be not afeared – the isle is full of noises,
> Sounds and sweet airs that give delight, and hurt not.
> Sometimes a thousand twangling instruments
> Will hum about mine ears; and sometimes voices
> That, if I then had waked after long sleep,
> Will make me sleep again; and then in dreaming,
> The clouds methought would open, and show riches
> Ready to drop upon me, that when I waked
> I cried to dream again.

The Old Vic is situated just along the road from a busy ambulance station. On the first night I got as far as, 'Be not afeared – the isle is full of noises,' and dead on cue came 'Doowah Doowah Doowah' as an ambulance sped up the Waterloo Road. The audience had hysterics of course, and I had to stop, turn my back, then fix them with a beady eye and start all over again. They loved it. Oddly enough, so did I.

That period from 1970 to 1975 was the last great golden sunset of Olivier's illustrious reign as actor-manager. It was filled with beauty, vigour and excitement, and was unquestionably the most rewarding period of my working life.

I wish we could have stayed at the Old Vic for ever, but she was crumbling about our ears, and our new home on the river was nearing completion. It was time to kiss the dear old lady goodbye and move on.

Chapter 9
Culture in Concrete

SEEN AT NIGHT across the river, from the gardens of the Victoria Embankment or from your suite at the Savoy, it looks glamorous and exciting – the huge dot matrix sign telling you of the delights on display in all three houses, light from the foyers and restaurants spilling out onto the balconies and terraces, the lovely old looped fairy lights along the riverside walk shining onto the newly planted plane trees – altogether an enchanting and seductive garden of delights, worthy of the majestic name 'Royal National Theatre'.

The approach by daylight from Waterloo station, however, is an altogether more richly variegated and challenging experience. Having recovered from your first view of the building, a vast, solid, window-less concrete cube, completely unadorned except by grubby rain streaks (which is, in fact, the flytower of the Lyttelton Theatre), you now have an interesting choice. You can take your courage in both hands and venture boldly into what Jonathan Miller christened The Mugger's Urinal, a dank netherworld of mind-numbing ugliness under the walkway to Waterloo Bridge, now inhabited mostly by macho teenage skateboarders who, being banned from the riverside, compensate by whizzing past you, millimetres away from your ankles, before performing incredibly skilful leaps and beautiful airborne *tours-en-l'air*, not always landing with the grace and precision of a Nureyev. If you survive this combined assault on your physical and mental stability, you will eventually arrive at the river and the coffee bar at the corner of the theatre, where a double espresso will pull you back together again.

If this seems too daunting, go the other way, along a perfectly ordinary unthreatening road on the opposite side of the building. As you stroll along in your best theatregoing clothes, looking forward to the civilised evening ahead of you, a delightful vista of the Thames gradually unfolds before you. You reach the corner, you turn it, and you stumble over a huge pile of empty beer-crates, bulging bin-bags and overflowing wheelie-bins. There is nowhere else for the kitchen staff to put all this stuff. Any idiot, of course, knows that the building should be designed so that this essential activity goes on somewhere at the back, unobserved by the patrons as they arrive, but Denys Lasdun got a knighthood for it, so he must know something about waste disposal that the rest of us haven't figured out. The moment you get past this little man-made mountain you are smashed in the face by the air-stream from the biggest extractor fan in London (or indeed anywhere else that I am aware of). Your ears are bombarded by a continuous roar, your nose by the aroma of leftover cabbage and stale cooking oil from a battery of chip-pans. You would like to back away a step or two, but inexplicably there is no side-walk here – nothing whatever between you and the 10-ton trucks, cars and tourist coaches which share this space with you. One impulsive step will land you under their wheels, and the choice between a noisome extractor fan and death under a bus is an easy one – stay with the smells.

You are now within a few yards of the front entrance. Ah – the front entrance. Where is it, exactly? On more than one occasion I have been asked by tourists for directions to the National Theatre when we were standing right in front of it. Walk up Shaftesbury Avenue and the names of all the theatres light up the night sky. Even here, on the South Bank, a sign across the frontage of the Festival Hall proudly proclaims its identity; a little further along, the IBM building leaves you in no doubt of its importance. But the big, grey concrete and glass building between them – what is that? The sign you saw from your suite in the Savoy is at the top of the building and invisible from the riverside, and there is nothing on the façade to tell you where you are – not one sign, *anywhere*, saying 'National Theatre'. There are some banners on the walkway which are very tall and very narrow and printed sideways, from bottom to top, so that if you lie down on your left side in the middle of the road on a calm, windless day, you can read the words 'Lyttelton' and 'Olivier' but there is no indication as to what these names mean, or where they can be found.

The way in *must* be through one of that impressive rank of glass doors facing you. The first two or three that you try bear the slogan: 'Out of use. Please use other door.' You do as bidden, and find one without the slogan. Opening it is another matter – it weighs more than any door you have ever encountered. Two strong young men could do it easily – a frail old lady could still be there the next morning, her hand frozen to the steel bar. You summon up your strength, get your son to help, and at last you are in. And miraculously, from now on, everything is wonderful.

The contrast with Shaftesbury Avenue could hardly be more extreme. The hour or so before curtain time in the foyer of any West End theatre is reminiscent of the Underground in the rush hour. Don't even *think* of trying to find somewhere to sit. Think instead, perhaps, of getting a drink. Squeezing between tightly packed bodies, treading on toes and apologising, you inch your way to within shouting distance of the bar. It will be a while before your shout is heard, though once it is, your drink will arrive with admirable speed; your only problem now is finding enough space to lift your elbow without knocking someone else's drink out of his hand.

Here at the National, you are in another world. A world of space, light, gaiety, relaxation and joyful anticipation. As you walk in through that recalcitrant door, you leave all the hassle behind, and enter a huge, impressive and – yes – beautiful space. To your left the bookshop is doing a brisk evening trade. Ahead of you a handsome staircase leads to the Mezzanine, the posh restaurant for dining before or after the show, and at the far end is a snack bar. Stretching across the wall opposite you is the Long Bar, which really is long and uncrowded; you take your drinks and join your friends at one of the plentiful tables scattered around, where hundreds of people are sitting in comfort with their pre-show drinks and savouring the splendid view across the river to Somerset House. Opposite the Long Bar is a raised platform with a grand piano, and at six o'clock a first-class classical or jazz group will play great music for an hour or so. It is hard to think of a better way to start an evening's entertainment.

What is it like when the bell rings and you move into the auditorium? Well, I cannot pretend to love the Lyttelton Theatre. It is a serviceable square box, all straight lines and confrontation, with very little rapport between the stage and the audience – in its own way it works, but I confess it is not my way.

The Olivier is another matter: a massive amphitheatre holding well over a thousand people, it offers the actor a warm embrace and a fierce challenge at the same time. The stage thrusts boldly out into the house; the front rows are within touching distance in front of you, beside you, and occasionally behind you, but at the far circumference of that great semi-circle a lot of people are a long, long way from you, and there are corners where the sound of the human voice does not want to go unless very firmly persuaded. Standing at the centre of this intensely focused arc of concentration and expectation can make you feel very small – or very powerful.

Some actors find it overwhelming and intimidating; I find it inspiring and liberating.

I love working in a big space which lets me move freely and boldly; I love the challenge of making the people at the back feel welcome and involved without those under my nose at the front feeling that I am ignoring them and going over their heads; I love to know that I am being heard in those distant pockets of sound-resistance without sounding as though I am shouting (thank you ,Ernst Urbach) and, surprisingly, given my aversion to concrete, I love the rugged unself-conscious beauty of the place. It is well named; like Olivier himself it is handsome, four square and strong, welcoming but demanding, with obvious faults but hugely compensating virtues. It has been a workplace for me, on and off, for over a quarter of a century, and I love it still.

Unfortunately, when we arrived in 1976, with Peter Hall's production of Albert Finney's *Hamlet*, in the very first season in the National's new home, and Peter in his first season as Director of the National, the Olivier was not ready – some building work was still to be done and the whole interior had to be fitted out – so we opened *Hamlet* in the Lyttelton instead, and then started rehearsing Marlowe's *Tamburlaine the Great*, which would eventually run in repertoire with *Hamlet* in the Olivier. While we worked, we waited for the building to be finished. We waited, and we waited – in fact we waited from March to October, and seven months is a long time to rehearse *Tamburlaine*, even when you are doing both Part I and Part II, as we were. (Thank God there isn't a Part III.) To keep us sane, we did some impromptu performances outside by the river which, besides giving us the chance to run the play for someone other than ourselves, gave the surprised strollers along the riverside a lot of unexpected fun, elicited some ribald loud-hailer comments from the guides on the river-boats, and stopped a lot of traffic on Waterloo Bridge. We even put on a production of *Troilus and Cressida* at the Young Vic, which kept us busy for a couple of months.

Then one memorable day Peter Hall gathered us all together and with a seraphic smile told us that at last, at *last*, he had been given a firm date for the completion of the Olivier, and we would be taking possession in a couple of weeks. We all cheered and hugged each other, and a minion walked in and whispered something in Peter's ear. The smile disappeared from that genial, cherubic face and was replaced by a contorted glare of wild, ungovernable rage. He flung his *Tamburlaine* script to the floor and jumped up and down on it quite a few times, turned on his heel and stalked out, seething with anger. There had been yet another delay, yet another strike by one or other of the unions involved, and our firm date was firm no longer.

Albert Finney, who was playing Tamburlaine as well as Hamlet and, to put it mildly, had a lot on his plate, was magnificent. I can think of many stars who, if they had not already walked out, would certainly have done so at this point, but Albert kept his cool, stuck to his guns and soldiered on, setting an example which restored everyone's spirits. An admirable display of company leadership.

Eventually, of course, all was well, and we opened both plays in the Olivier.

As Bajazeth, the mighty emperor captured by Tamburlaine, I was imprisoned in an iron cage, and had to kill myself by beating my brains out on the bars. A concoction of red poster paint and black-currant jam filled one of the hollow bars, and as I bashed my head I activated a little pump on the bar with my thumb and this wonderfully gooey mixture poured all over my forehead and ran down my face onto the floor. It was very effective – so much so that one night a woman in the front row moaned weakly, 'Oh my God!' and fainted, distracting the audience's attention from my brilliantly blood-curdling death throes while she was carried, limp and unconscious, to the nearest exit.

To our intense relief, both productions were extremely successful after all those months of stress and uncertainty, and my long love affair with the Olivier had begun. The consummation of that affair, however, was delayed for a few years by a gratifying series of irresistible offers from other places. First, the Royal Shakespeare Company presented me with a 24-carat gift in the shape of Terri Dennis, the adorable drag queen in Peter Nichols' dazzling *Privates on Parade*, playing opposite the late, great Nigel Hawthorne, with the best director of them all, Michael Blakemore, who had directed me in *Long Day's Journey*, *The Front Page*, *Macbeth* and *The Cherry Orchard* during the great Olivier years at the Old Vic. This was an offer which I couldn't refuse, and as well as earning me an Olivier award, it also earned me the distinction of being, so far as I am aware, the first actor ever to work simultaneously for the National and the RSC, as I was still playing in *Hamlet* and *Tamburlaine* while rehearsing *Privates on Parade*.

Then Eddie Kulukundis asked me if I would like to play opposite Deborah Kerr as her husband in Bernard Shaw's *Candida*. Would I like to? Yes, I thought I really would rather like to – wouldn't you? Deborah, the sweetest and kindest of ladies, had not a bad word to say about anyone in the entire world except Charlton Heston. When I asked her why, she replied: 'No giggles.' She had played *Long Day's Journey* with Heston in Los Angeles, and: 'We rehearsed for six whole weeks and never once did we have a giggle. It was all "the architectonics of the motivation" or "This scene is playing thirty seconds longer than it did yesterday." It was so damned serious I could have screamed.'

Well, we had a few giggles with *Candida*. On Deborah's birthday we decided that this great love of hers for Chuck Heston would be properly celebrated. While she and I were on stage playing the last scene, Maureen Lipman, who was playing my secretary, papered every square inch of the walls of Deborah's dressing room with about three hundred photographs of You-know-who, and hung up a banner which stretched across the whole width of the room saying HAPPY BIRTHDAY DEBORAH, with a picture of Chuck smiling shyly through every letter. I am sure her screams of delighted laughter as she came through the door were heard by the departing customers in the auditorium.

During rehearsals she and I used to go to the local pub for lunch. Michael Blakemore (yes – him again) who doesn't like pubs, didn't join us, and when we returned for the afternoon session he would greet us with a sardonically raised eyebrow, and in that suave, almost imperceptibly Australian voice would say: 'Are we in a fit state to do two or three hours' work, then?' So, when we did a newspaper interview together one day, we got the photographer to take a picture of us looking as debauched as possible, fags on the go, pints in hand, eyes crossed, and presented Michael with it on the opening night. He was amused and delighted, and the image of Deborah Kerr the prim English rose took another welcome knock.

Not long after this joyful collaboration came to an end, another very different but equally enjoyable treat came my way. I was about to leave for Los Angeles to film some interiors for a movie, when the American producer/director Hal Prince rang out of the blue. I didn't think he was aware of my existence, but he must have seen and liked some of my work because his words were:

'I hear you're on your way to LA. Why don't you stop by in New York and see *Sweeney Todd*? See what you think.'

So I stopped by, I saw *Sweeney Todd*, and what did I think?

I was knocked over backwards in my seat by the power, beauty, wit and terror of this musical masterpiece by Stephen Sondheim. Unlike some of his works (*Into the Woods*, *Sunday in the Park with George*) in which the promise of the first half is not always, to my ear, entirely fulfilled in the second, *Sweeney* builds inexorably, though with plenty of time for comedy and exquisite lyrical interludes on the way, to a shattering climax which for me has no equal in musical theatre. And for those who say that Sondheim's shows have 'no tunes,' I must tell them that they astonish me, and assure them that *Sweeney* is bursting with beautiful songs and beautiful orchestral sequences, and melodies that Andrew Lloyd Webber would die for.

This is true of many of Sondheim's other shows as well, and to say, as many do, that his music is arid and intellectual is to miss the point. It is useless to complain that he is not Jerry Herman. As will become clear shortly, I yield to none in my love and admiration for Herman, who, apparently effortlessly and spontaneously, writes irresistibly infectious melodies and lyrics which deliver laughter, sadness, charm and love straight down the middle in time-honoured Broadway fashion. He doesn't try (or need to try) to do what Sondheim does by nature. I know them both and they are *very* different men. George-Louis de Buffon, an eighteenth-century French naturalist of whom I know absolutely nothing apart from this, wrote 'Le style, c'est l'homme même' – the style is the man himself. These two could no more change their style than change their own natures. Sondheim's intricate and fascinating quasi-recitatives, which Herman would leave as spoken dialogue, gradually lead from speech rhythms to the point where poetry must take over, and when the big tunes come they are gorgeous.

For the first preview of *Sweeney* at Drury Lane in 1980, our son David, who was now eleven, was given two seats in a stage box to watch the show with a school friend. As I rose scarily up from my grave, singing:

Attend the tale of Sweeney Todd
His skin was pale and his eye was odd
He shaved the faces of gentlemen
Who never thereafter were heard of again...

he leaned across to his friend, and in a fortissimo stage whisper said: 'That's my Dad!' The front stalls gave him a round of applause.

The actual opening night got off to what you might call a cracking start. An important element in the enormous and somewhat over-elaborate stage-setting was a massive steel gantry which rose and fell during the course of the action depending on whether it was depicting a passage to the Judge's house, a warders' gallery in a madhouse, or an escape route for the young lovers. For the first scene – my return to London after fifteen years of deportation in Australia – it was lowered to become a bridge over the Thames. Lowered, as it happened, on this occasion a few feet too far. I rowed my little boat across the stage, singing lustily how good it was to be home again, and as I reached the climactic line: 'Oh, there's no place like London!' I rose energetically to my feet, spreading my arms wide to encompass the view, and smashed my head onto twenty tons of solid steel. I dropped like a stone onto my seat, and my companion in the little boat held me up straight while the vast Drury Lane auditorium went round in circles and my brain was muttering: 'Christ, what a way to play a Press Night – knock yourself out in scene one!' Fortunately I was wearing a rather fetching woolly hat with a bobble on top which softened the blow enough for me to carry on, with a pained expression on my face which I fondly hoped conveyed to the audience my rage and frustration at being exiled in Australia for so long.

Half-way through the run we did a special Gala Night performance. I forget what it was in aid of, but I do remember that among the invited dignitaries was Harold Wilson, looking rather miffed at not being allowed to smoke his pipe in the middle of the stalls. Mr Todd's Tonsorial Parlour was upstairs above Mrs Lovett's Pie Shop, and a lever on the barber's chair activated an ingenious mechanism which, after I had cut my customers' throats, whizzed them smoothly down a chute into Sheila Hancock's kitchen, where she turned them smartly into meat pies. My last customer of all was the hated Judge who had seduced my wife and sent me to Australia, and his come-uppance was the beginning of the build-up to the great final climax. A fairly important moment. (Incidentally, the blood spurting from his throat had much the same effect several times on ladies in the front rows as my brain-bashing had in *Tamburlaine*.) On this Gala Night, after triumphantly cutting the Judge's throat, I pulled the magic lever – and nothing happened. I kept on singing and saw the stage manager in the wings performing an elaborate mime-show worthy of Marcel Marceau which I took to mean that the mechanism had failed, and some other method of disposal was required. I glanced down where she pointed upstage of the little house and saw four burly stage-hands standing in a row with their arms out, nodding and smiling. I whispered in the Judge's ear: 'You're going off the top, mate.' 'Oh, Jesus!' came the strangled reply, and he went as stiff as a board – surely a record speed for the onset of rigor mortis? I lugged him out of the chair to the back of the set, noticing as I went the conductor still waving his baton with his mouth wide open and eyes popping out of his head, made it to the back and hurled him over the edge safely into those waiting arms. A huge round of applause from the audience, of course – I seem to have spent much of my career getting ovations for things that go disastrously wrong.

Sweeney won another Olivier award for me, and the *Evening Standard* award for Stephen. He rang me from New York, asking me to accept it on his behalf, which of course I did with great pride. Some months later, when he was back in London after *Sweeney* had closed, he invited me to dinner and asked me to bring the statuette with me. I knew that his latest show *Merrily We Roll Along* had recently opened on Broadway and failed, and that he was disappointed that *Sweeney* had not run longer. I also knew that he was prone to black depressions and would certainly be feeling very low. I had a rough tape recording of the last night of *Sweeney* at Drury Lane, at which he had not been present, and I set up a few sections which I thought were good, with the singing and acting going well and lots of laughter and applause from the audience, including the whole of the climactic final scene, with Sweeney making his final exit through a great metal door upstage centre and slamming the door shut on the very last note of music, at which the audience erupted into wild cheering and stamping, and threw roses onto the stage.

I arrived at the apartment near Marble Arch where he was staying with his friend the lyricist Burt Shevelove, I presented him with his *Evening Standard* statuette, and I sat him down and started the tape. As it played, the frown lines on his face gradually softened, and an almost imperceptible lift at the corners of his mouth grew into a ravishing smile of pure happiness, his depression visibly, almost tangibly, lifted, and tears (of joy, honestly) plopped onto the statuette sitting on his lap. Those who decry his so-called lack of emotion should have been there. After that we had a very happy evening. He had to believe me about the roses, of course – I don't think anyone has found a way to record the sound of a flower landing on an actor's foot, especially with two thousand people roaring approval at the same time.

It was fascinating and instructive to step straight from this into the utterly different world of Jerry Herman and discover at first hand, from the inside, the immense skill and emotional understanding which goes into those songs which seem so simple. They are indeed simple, but it is the simplicity of genius. We were trying out *Mack and Mabel* at the Nottingham Playhouse; I was playing Mack and we saw several girls in our search for a Mabel. One of them stood out like a shining little jewel, a very young and completely unknown Imelda Staunton. She was shy and she was nervous but her emotional honesty and the simple truth of her acting set her completely apart, and her singing, even then, was most beautiful. We cast her without hesitation. The production went very well, Imelda was wonderful as Mabel, and Duncan Weldon came to see it with a view to taking it to the West End. He took me out to supper and, worrying about costs as producers always do, asked me if I thought the cast or the orchestra could be made any smaller. I told him truthfully that we were already down to the irreducible minimum, so he went back to London and instead of putting us into theatre he had free, he put in Dave Allen. One man and one chair – that's as small a cast as you can get – though admittedly Dave Allen had enough talent for six.

So our *Mack and Mabel* didn't make it to London. If it had, it would have made Imelda a star overnight. She is a star now, of course, but it would have given her a lovely kick-start. Someone tried to revive it in the West End a few years ago, but made the disastrous, fatal mistake of casting Mack as a handsome young leading man looking much the same age as his Mabel, who sang 'I Won't Send Roses' as a straight romantic love song. (No – this is not sour grapes,

Top: John Gielgud and DQ on the set of *Murder on the Orient Express*, 1974.

Bottom: Joe Melia, DQ and Simon Jones in the film version of *Privates on Parade*, 1982.

Above: DQ and Deborah Kerr act up during the run of *Candida*, 1977.

Top left: DQ in *Rhinestone Cowboy*, 1979. *Top right:* DQ and SQ, 1975.

Bottom: DQ, Anthony Quayle, Peter O'Toole, Clive Francis and Anthony Valentine on the set of *Masada*, 1981.

Above: DQ in *Sweeney Todd*, 1980.

© Catherine Ashmore

Photographer unknown

Top: George Hearn and DQ in *La Cage aux Folles*, 1986.
Bottom: David Healey, SQ, DQ, George and Lesley Hearn, 1986.

Top left: DQ and Diana Rigg in *Antony and Cleopatra*, 1985. *Top right:* Liz Robertson and DQ in *My Fair Lady*, 1988.

Bottom: SQ and DQ at the SWET awards, mid-1980s.

Top: James Mason, Jane Birkin, Maggie Smith and DQ in *Evil Under the Sun*, 1981.

Bottom: Pierce Brosnan and DQ in *Mister Johnson*, 1990.

Top left: Jack Klaff, DQ and Tim Pigott-Smith in publicity for *The Royal Hunt of the Sun*, 1989. *Top right:* DQ in *A Patriot for Me*, 1995.

Bottom: DQ as Falstaff in *The Merry Wives of Windsor*, 1995.

Top: DQ and Susannah Harker in *She Stoops to Conquer*, 1992.
Bottom: DQ and Alun Armstrong in *Sweeney Todd*, 1993.

XXV

© Alastair Muir

© Catherine Ashmore/National Theatre

© Catherine Ashmore (National Theatre)

Top left: DQ as Prospero in *The Tempest*, 1996. *Top Right:* DQ in *Candide*, 1999.

Bottom: Oliver Cotton, Roger Allam, Mark Umbers, DQ and David Weston in *Troilus and Cressida*, 1999.

© John Haynes

© Robert Day

© Clive Barda/ArenaPAL

Top: Greg Hicks and DQ in *Waiting for Godot*, 1997.
Bottom left: DQ in *Brief Candle*, 1999.
Bottom right: DQ in *Racing Demon*, 1998.

Top: Cathryn Bradshaw, John Caird, Diana Rigg, Simon Russell Beale, Marcia Warren and DQ in rehearsal for *Humble Boy*, 2001.

Bottom: The same scene in performance, 2001.

© Catherine Ashmore

© Catherine Ashmore

Top: DQ and Simon Russell Beale in *Hamlet*, 2000.
Bottom: DQ in *Anything Goes*, 2002.

Photographer unknown (Christopher Fry)

Photographer unknown

Top: SQ, Christopher Fry and DQ, 2000.
Bottom: DQ's English teacher Don Francombe, DQ and SQ, 1995.

XXX

Top: DQ with accompanist Carol Wells performing *The Best of Times*, 1990s.
Bottom left: DQ in rehearsals for *Candide*, 1999.
Bottom right: DQ with granddaughter Hayley, 1998.

Top: The Quilley family, 1990. Hayley, David, Joanna, Sarah, SQ and DQ.
Bottom: The OBE investiture, 2002. Joanna, DQ, SQ and David.

folks, because by then I was much too old for the part – it would have looked like paedophilia.) The whole point of this relationship is that Mabel, a nineteen- or twenty-year-old waitress from the corner deli, falls in love with a man old enough to be her father, a man obsessed with his work, used to getting his own way, self-sufficient and a bit of a bully. She cooks him a veal supper like her mother used to make, and tentatively wonders wouldn't it be nice if they could be a Proper Couple, like other people?

'You're a nice kid, Mabel,' he replies, 'and your veal and peppers ain't bad. I don't mind spending a little time with you, just so long as you understand the rules.' And then sings:

> I won't send roses
> Or hold the door
> I won't remember
> Which dress you wore …

He sings a whole (beautiful) song about what a rude son-of-a-bitch he is and how she should stay away from him, until, with the very last line of all, he sings:

> I won't send roses
> And roses suit you so.

It is an enchanting musical cameo of a tough middle-aged man falling in love with a girl half his age without meaning to, and almost without realising it.

Sondheim and Herman, incidentally, are among the select band of composers who write their own lyrics – like the great Frank Loesser and Cole Porter, with whom they can both, in their own way, bear comparison. They are at opposite ends of the great and glorious rainbow spectrum of American musical theatre. We need them both.

Five movies and five television shows filled the next five years, and then something much more exciting and important happened: I was reunited with my Old Dutch. Let me rephrase that: the beautiful and talented Diana Rigg swanned elegantly back into my life, to play Cleopatra to my Antony at the Chichester Festival.

We had had our first skirmish back in the '60s when *The Avengers* was top of the TV Pops and Diana as Emma Peel was every man's pin-up girl. I was playing a young RAF officer who fancied his chances with her, and she dampened my ardour by grabbing me in a judo hold and hurling me through the air to land in a crumpled heap on the floor. To be honest, the flying through the air bit was done by a stuntman in my uniform, but the crumpled heap on the floor was all me. Although this was certainly an interesting start to the first of our many collaborations, it hardly qualifies as a picture of us as what Mabel would have called a Proper Couple. But over the years, that was what we were to become. We were the Macbeths at the Old Vic in 1972; we were an engaged couple in the film of *In This House of Brede* in '75 (she left me to become a nun – can you imagine?); we were Agamemnon and Clytemnestra in *The Serpent Son*, the BBC's TV version of the *Oresteia*; we were married in Agatha Christie's *Evil Under the Sun* – six lovely weeks in Mallorca – and now we were to be Antony and Cleopatra.

Many years later, at the National, we were girlfriend and boyfriend (well, lady friend and gentleman friend) in Charlotte Jones' delightful *Humble Boy*. We were such a comfortable couple by that time that when Diana was asked to supply biographical notes for the programme of *Humble Boy* (the bit that usually reads: 'She began her career at Smalltown Rep, and progressed to small parts in...' etc, etc) she said, 'Oh, I can't be bothered with all that' and her entire entry read:

DIANA RIGG. Diana Rigg has been around for a very long time, and this is the sixth time that she has coupled with Denis Quilley.

There were a few envious men in that audience.

We were good together as Antony and Cleopatra, and Norman Rodway, who died much too young a few years ago, was the most marvellous Enobarbus – tough, cynical, intelligent, vulnerable, with what Stella described as a smile like a razor.

There seems to be a little God of Drama sitting somewhere on Parnassus who decrees that whenever I play a really butch, tough bruiser it must be followed as soon as possible by a sweet old queen. The mighty emperor Bajazeth in *Tamburlaine* was nimbly usurped by the ineffable Terri Dennis in *Privates on Parade*; Antony was smoothly upstaged by Georges, half of a lovely gay couple in *La Cage aux Folles*, and some years later Sweeney Todd (in the revival at the National) was given a good seeing-off by Baron von Epp, the transvestite swinger in *A Patriot for Me*.

Jerry Herman's musical *La Cage aux Folles* was another of the great, unforgettable highlights of my theatrical life, along with *The Front Page*, *Long Day's Journey*, *Sweeney Todd* and *Privates on Parade*. The French film on which it was based was a small, domestic, romantic comedy about Georges, who runs the nightclub of the title, and his gay partner Albin, who is the club's star drag artist. Some time in his misspent youth Georges had managed to father a son, who turns up halfway through, creating a certain amount of mayhem, but basically the film concentrated on the bickering but loving relationship between the two middle-aged men.

The musical was still playing with great success on Broadway, and its director, the great writer/director and all-round man of the theatre Arthur Laurents persuaded the producers to fly us to New York and put us up for a few days so that we could see the show and get acquainted with George Hearn, who was playing Albin and would be my partner in London. As Stella and I walked to the theatre on the first evening in New York I was full of doubts – I was desperately concerned that this fragile little masterpiece of film would be vulgarised and inflated by the inevitable demands of a Broadway show, and that the gentle sweetness at its heart would be lost.

I should not have worried. Jerry Herman had performed the miraculous feat of turning this little gem into a big, camp, colourful musical filled with great songs, glamour and spectacle in the most lavish straight-down-the-line Broadway manner, but punctuated with moments of exquisite poignancy, and somehow managing to preserve unharmed the simplicity and the tenderness of the central relationship between Georges and Albin. I sat and watched, feeling totally, ridiculously happy, and the happiness was confirmed and deepened when we met George Hearn afterwards. George at that time was, like me, an established leading man without being an internationally known star. Like me he had done a bit of everything – rep, Shakespeare, musicals, concerts, television; and like me he had no interest in 'celebrity' – the quality of the work and the congeniality of his colleagues was everything. We became instant friends, and I *knew* we would work well together in London.

In the event we did – and more. The respect and affection we felt for each other created a warm ambience which pervaded the whole company and crew. A good relationship at the top *always* percolates down and spreads an aura of friendliness, happiness and enjoyment throughout the production. Audiences sense this immediately and are warmed by it, sometimes without realising how or why. With

Arthur Laurents' expert guidance every character was brilliantly played, but I think our greatest achievement was the creation of that intangible atmosphere of joy. Of the hundreds of appreciative letters I received during the run, nearly all of them ended saying something like: 'We left feeling six feet off the ground' or: 'It really cheered me up' or, best of all: 'It was such a loving show.'

In his latter years, Larry Olivier became increasingly frail and occasionally a little vague, but he was still quite capable of ordering people about. He was living in a little house in the country now, and he would ring up and say:

'Can yer come down and see me? I'm lonely. Joanie's working in Town and I've only got the nurse and driver. Grab hold of Stella and get yerselves down here for lunch.'

Lunch, of course, meant the afternoon as well, then a bit of dinner and an evening of rambling reminiscing. One evening we were talking about Keith Michell, who had left his native Adelaide to work in the Young Vic with me in 1950.

'I brought him over here, yer know, gave him his first job in London.' That surprised me a bit. 'Nice feller, but then of course he had that affair with Vivien, and we couldn't be friends any more.'

Light dawned on me: 'Oh – Peter Finch, you mean.'

'Yes, that's right, Australian feller. What's he doing now?'

I hadn't the heart to tell him that Finchie was dead and that it wasn't him we were talking about, but another Australian feller. However, despite these little lapses of memory, he was still in good form, and great company.

After opening the new Lilian Baylis studio theatre at Sadler's Wells with John Guare's quirky and fascinating *House of Blue Leaves*, Stella and I took a quick break in our little flat in Marbella. As I swam lazily towards the edge of the pool, an excited neighbour ran over and called to me:

'Have you heard?'

'Heard what?'

'Laurence Olivier has died.'

The poor lady had no idea of the effect her words would have. She helped me up the steps, apologising for her clumsiness, but in truth it would have been the same however the news arrived. It was the 11th July 1989. A great blazing fire had gone out, and a huge, rich chapter of theatrical history had finally closed.

I was asked to be an usher at the memorial service in Westminster Abbey, but by then it was October and I was on tour in *The Royal Hunt of the Sun*, Peter Shaffer's epic play about Pizarro and Atahualpa. This was for Compass Theatre, an excellent touring company created and run by Anthony Quayle, another great pillar of the theatrical establishment. He was unwell at the time, and this production had been expertly directed by Tim Piggott-Smith.

On the day of Larry's memorial service we were in Belfast, and unable to get to the service I was just settling down to watch it on television in my room in the much-bombed Europa Hotel, when the company manager came in and told me that Tony Quayle had died.

It is a grossly overworked phrase, but really and truly that was the end of an era.

Chapter 10
The Fleeting Image

THE ASTUTE READER (if he is still with me) will have noticed by now that films and television have hardly been mentioned so far. There are two reasons for this: firstly I have tried to present a coherent and roughly chronological picture of a lifetime in the theatre without too many diversions, except of a personal nature; secondly (and, let's face it, this is the *real* reason) I have always felt that live theatre is my proper job, the stage is my home, and my forays onto the screen, large and small, have been enjoyable excursions which helped to reduce my overdraft and took me to some fascinating places, but somehow were never part of the real work. It is a little surprising, then, to look back and see how much screen work I seem to have done.

Sarah Pond is a long-standing member of my small but devoted group of faithful fans, and when I rang her to check a couple of dates she revealed that she had a list of every single thing I had ever done – theatre, TV, concerts, movies, everything – with all the dates and locations. She gave me a copy, and it has been a godsend for me, disorganised and forgetful as I am, in putting these memoirs in some sort of order. Thank you, Sarah!

The leader of this loyal little band of supporters, Pam Remnant, got them all kitted out in white T-shirts adorned with a red rose and the legend 'Denis Quilley Appreciation Society'. (She gave me one too, but I have to be very careful who sees me wearing it.) One night they all came to see *La Cage aux Folles* at the Palladium. They had all seen it before on various occasions, but this time they had decided to come en masse. The Cagelles, our dancing boys and girls, had christened my fans The Quillettes, and as they came dancing off into the wings that night, chief Cagelle Scott St Martin whispered in my ear: 'The Quillettes are here in force tonight, dear – it's an absolute *sea* of white T-shirts out there' and did a cheeky grand jeté off to his dressing room.

Sarah's Great List informed me that I had appeared in about 100 plays in the theatre, 54 one-night stands of various kinds (concerts, one-man shows, charity galas, etc) and 25 LPs and CDs of musicals. Well, no great surprises there, but it also reminded me, to my astonishment that I had done 15 movies, 54 TV dramas (some of which ran for anything from 6 to 26 episodes, and no less than 74 other TV appearances – several editions of *This is your Life* (including my own), interviews, chat shows, award ceremonies and so on, plus nine times on *Call my Bluff* and – the jewel in the crown – nine times as the star of the Crinkly Bottom Amateur Dramatic Society in *Noel's House Party*. You may laugh, but this was always a hugely enjoyable day. Noel Edmonds was the most genial and charming of hosts, Tony Britton was usually there, in his running character as a High Court Judge, and the mystery guests were always fun to be with. The rehearsals were relaxed and giggly, the show itself was absolutely daft but ridiculously enjoyable, and the great thing was that it was *live* – probably one of the reasons I enjoyed it so much. Noel was totally relaxed in charge of all the mayhem, his rapport with the live audience was warm and spontaneous, and nothing made him lose his cool. If anything went wrong he was instantly ready with an ad lib and a joke, completely imperturbable.

Of course, when I first worked in television, in the early '50s, *everything* was live; there was no videotape, and no way of recording a programme. If there was a repeat of a play, and there usually was, you came back to the studio next week and did it all over again.

Quick costume changes had to be done without holding the action up, and if you went offstage left at the end of one scene and had to enter stage right for the next in a different costume, there was a lot of running round behind wobbly sets, and probably a bit of ad-libbing from your colleagues until you arrived late, breathless and still zipping up your flies.

Many years later something called tele-recording arrived, but you still had to play the show straight through because the process of stopping, going back and restarting was, for some obscure technical reason, fiendishly expensive. So fluffs and dries and minor cock-ups tended to be left in. If you were in a really serious hole, the only way to make the people in the control booth press the dreaded Stop Button was to look straight into the lens and shout: 'Oh, *bugger* it!' or some more powerful four-letter expletive, which gave the poor devils absolutely no choice. It was all very primitive and rough, but there was a dangerous excitement about it, like a first-night adrenalin rush, which is completely lost with the safety of pre-recording.

Another surprise for me was the range and high quality of the material in the TV shows I appeared in during the '50s, '60s and '70s. Everything from *Dixon of Dock Green* and *The Avengers*, a Francis Durbridge thriller, a Sherlock Holmes story and an opera by Carl Davis based on *Les Liaisons Dangereuses*, up to a quite extraordinary number of great dramatic masterpieces: *The Merchant of Venice*, Pirandello's *Henry IV*, T S Eliot's *Murder in the Cathedral*, O'Neill's *Long Day's Journey into Night*, *Agamemnon* by Aeschylus, Arthur Miller's *The Crucible*, and more. It's hard to imagine one of those great plays being given three hours of prime time on television today – potential sponsors and advertisers would roar with laughter or run away screaming. I wonder what the ratings would be? They could just possibly be a lot higher than the money men might think.

My very first encounter with a TV studio was in 1951, when the new medium was just beginning to take off, and people used to crowd together outside electrical stores to watch a flickering little postcard size black and white image through the shop window. We were in the studio to play *The Black Arrow*, which for me was probably an unfortunate introduction to the small screen, as it was a play we had been touring for some months with the Young Vic. This meant that instead of starting to learn a new technique from scratch with a new play and a clean slate, I had to remodel something which was well-entrenched in its original form, and try to make it work in a new and unfamiliar way. I felt confused and restricted by the need to make all the movements and gestures smaller and subtler, having to use much less vocal projection in order to make the dialogue more naturalistic, and having to restage a lot of the action so that the unwieldy cameras could do what the very basic shooting plot demanded, and squeeze three actors, who on stage had been twenty feet apart, into one rather densely populated shot.

I got used to it in time, of course, and even became quite good at it, but it was never going to become a serious or well-loved part of my life. A pity in a way, because unless they've seen you On The Telly, most people think you've retired, or died, or emigrated. (Or, of course, they've never heard of you.)

Movies presented problems of an entirely different kind. Worst of all was the complete lack of proper rehearsal. By the time I first got into films I had already been working in the theatre for twenty years; the working rhythm was part of my nature, and the one crucial, indispensable element in that rhythm was the rehearsal period. Whether it lasts for one week or six the basic principle is the same. You have had the script for some time beforehand, you know your way around it and you have a rough idea (perhaps even quite a clear idea) of how your part should go and how it fits into the piece as a whole. On the first day you meet all your fellow-actors; some of them are probably old friends, some you are meeting for the first time. You read the play through from beginning to end, listening hard to the other actors, and already some of your ideas are looking as if they might change, as you hear different thoughts and spontaneous reactions coming from several directions. This process continues throughout rehearsal, minds changing, new discoveries being made, right up to the opening night.

Then the first time you play it to an audience their reaction gives you more new ideas, and as that reaction subtly varies from one night to another, so does your timing and, sometimes, the depth of feeling in your delivery of a line. This was demonstrated to me brilliantly and forcefully during the run of *Long Day's Journey* at the Old Vic. Larry Olivier played my father, and he and I had a scene in which he tells me that the Doctor has confirmed that my younger brother has consumption and will have to go into a sanatorium.

> ME: Well, for God's sake pick out a good place and not some cheap dump.
> LARRY: I'll send him wherever Dr Hardy thinks best.
> ME: What I'm afraid of is, with your Irish bog-trotter idea that consumption is fatal, you'll figure it would be a waste of money to spend any more than you can help.
> LARRY: You liar!
> ME: All right. Prove I'm a liar. That's what I want. That's why I brought it up.

There was usually a slight, almost inaudible reaction from the audience after my jibe about not wanting to spend more than he could help, but Larry always rode over it without pausing and played

'You liar' firmly and dismissively but quietly and without over-emphasis. One night, however, my line for some reason prompted a big mass intake of breath followed by a sort of 'Ooh,' meaning 'What a terrible thing to say'. Larry heard it and instantly capitalised on it. Instead of going straight on, he leaned back in his chair and fixed me malevolently with those armour-piercing eyes for a very long and scary ten seconds before blasting me with a long-drawn-out, 'You LIAR!!' I had a non-second to decide whether to play my reply loud and strong as usual – no, no good going up, I couldn't top that, so I went down, and said, 'All right – prove I'm a liar,' quietly and sardonically. It worked, and the scene had turned on a sixpence in a new direction. 'That was fun, wasn't it?' he grinned as we came off.

One of the great joys of my job is that you are never alone. You can't act in a vacuum; your every action provokes a reaction, every thought and emotion bounces off your partner and comes back imbued with his thought and emotion, as you build the scene together. When we are up there on stage we know that we depend entirely on each other. I believe this makes most actors into generous, unselfish and supportive people. I am not talking about 'celebrities' here, I am talking about actors. There is a popular notion that all actors are bitchy and egotistical, and that the profession is a back-stabbing rat-race. This is simply not true. I have known (and admired) many writers and composers over the years, and I have often found them to be very critical and dismissive about their peers. Just recently, for example, the Booker Prize-winning novelist A S Byatt launched a long article on the internet denigrating J K Rowling and the Harry Potter books. She said that Rowling lacks the skill of the great children's writers, and that she is baffled as to why Rowling is read by so many adults. Of the latest volume she writes:

It is written for people whose imaginative lives are confined to TV cartoons and the exaggerated mirror worlds of soaps, reality TV and celebrity gossip. Some adult Harry Potter fans are simply reverting to the child they were when they read Billy Bunter or Enid Blyton. They are inhabitants of urban jungles, not the real world. They don't have the skill to tell ersatz magic from the real thing.

Now I have never read a word of the Harry Potter books, so for all I know everything she says may be perfectly true. But that is not the point. What is really unpleasant is the meanness (and jealousy?) behind such a vitriolic assault, in the most public way possible, on a fellow-member of Byatt's own profession. I am sure that this is due, at least in part, to the fact that writers work alone, with only themselves as a sounding-board, and inevitably become self-centred, whereas actors work as a team. And you must believe me when I say that actors positively enjoy praising other actors' work. Can you imagine Simon Russell Beale slagging off Anthony Sher on the internet, and saying that his work only appeals to people of low intelligence and no imagination? No, of course not – it is absolutely unthinkable. Nor is it true that most actors are shallow and unintelligent – another popular misconception which is not helped by the inane prattlings of 'celebrities' who think that being famous for going to lots of parties and being photographed for *Hello* magazine qualifies them for a serious and difficult job. At the risk of seeming self-regarding, I cannot resist quoting the distinguished novelist and chronicler of London, Peter Ackroyd:

Having met a few actors I discover that they are much more intelligent than writers, much more alive and sympathetic, and alert and quick-witted too.

Well, I wouldn't dare go as far as that myself, but I do think that, although perhaps a *trifle* overstated, it is a pleasing tribute to a sometimes underrated profession.

All of the above may seem irrelevant when we are supposed to be talking about films, but I hope it will help to explain why I feel so strongly about the lack of rehearsal in moviemaking. The only film I ever made which *was* properly rehearsed was *Murder on the Orient Express*, directed by the great Sidney Lumet, who not only persuaded an incredible array of stars to play comparatively small parts (Sean Connery, Lauren Bacall, Richard Widmark, Vanessa Redgrave, John Gielgud, Albert Finney, Ingrid Bergman, Wendy Hiller – oh, and Colin Blakely and Denis Quilley) but also managed to get every one of them to rehearse for an unprecedented ten days before shooting started. This, naturally, saved a huge amount of very expensive studio time, and meant that he brought the film in under-time and under-budget, thereby saving the bacon of a studio which was in serious financial difficulties. He was not only completely on top of everything technical – lighting, lenses, camera angles, etc – he was also a sensitive director for the actors, always willing to suggest motivations, listen to problems and offer helpful advice. The ultimate pro.

The other disconcerting thing about filming, if you are new to the game, is that you never shoot in story-order, starting at the beginning and finishing at the end. For logistical and financial reasons scenes are grouped together according to the location in which they are set. So you spend a week or so shooting all the scenes set in, let's say, the leading man's flat, even though those scenes are scattered throughout the story, then all the scenes in his office, then all the scenes in his girlfriend's country house, and so on. This means that ninety-nine times out of a hundred you start shooting in the middle of the story, with only a hazy idea of the pace or atmosphere or intensity of the half-hour that will lead up to this point in the finished move. Tony Quayle gave me some good advice when I asked him how he coped with this.

'You have two options,' he said. 'Either you trust your director implicitly and do exactly as he says every day, or you spend some time before shooting starts working out the shape of your part, on your own or with someone listening and cueing you, and find out where the climaxes are, which are the funny bits and which the sad bits, until you've got an interpretation that makes sense to *you*, then you can do a scene anywhere in the story, in any order, and you are in a strong position to take notes and suggestions from the director.' You can guess which option I chose.

My first movie, in 1965, was called *Where the Spies Are*, a sort of sub-Bond caper starring David Niven. I had just one scene, as a dentist implanting a miniature microphone into one of Mr Niven's teeth, and trying to deliver witty and insouciant dialogue at the same time. I was terrified. Quite apart from it being my first day ever on a film set, the thought of damaging that million-dollar smile and holding up production while it was repaired at ruinous expense turned my brain to mush and my fingers to trembling clumsy sausages. A real dentist had taken me very quickly and sketchily through the motions (without a real mouth to practice on) and was watching to check the authenticity of the procedure – though I cannot imagine that he had spent much of his distinguished career sticking microphones into molars. His contribution during the shoot consisted of shouting:

'Cut! You can't put the wet cottonwool plug in your bloody *pocket*!' and similar encouraging little hints about once a minute. Somehow I survived this nightmare and eventually managed the whole scene in one uninterrupted take. Niven said, 'Bravo, well done,' in a voice that conveyed more relief than enthusiasm, and I gratefully retreated, shaking and sweating, to the sanctuary of my dressing room.

Anne of the Thousand Days was a doddle by comparison. I greatly enjoyed playing scenes with Richard Burton, whom I had understudied in the theatre twenty years before, and I was filled with amazement and admiration at the amount of booze he managed to put away without impairing his performance. He would start, literally, in the make-up chair at eight in the morning and carry on steadily throughout the day. Never drunk, just nicely topped up. (As Spencer Tracy once said: 'Just enough of a bun on to shield me from the harsh realities of life.') Richard's entourage were so well trained that even if we were shooting in a field in the middle of nowhere he only had to snap his fingers and say 'Bloody Mary' and zoom – it was in his hand. Only once was he caught on the hop. At lunchtime one day he was told that they were almost certain he was finished for the day, but would he mind staying on call just in case? At five o'clock it was decided there was just time to take a long-shot of us all returning from a deer-hunt. If you look closely at the head of the column, in front of the dead deer dangling from a pole, you will see Brook Williams and myself, each with a discreet hand under an elbow, steering our leader in the right direction and making sure he stays upright.

A typical day in a film studio is quite remarkably boring: half an hour's work on the set followed by two hours waiting in your dressing-room while the lights and cameras are set up, with your stand-in walking your moves, then a quarter of an hour on the set, and an hour and a half waiting, and so on throughout a very long day. But, in total contrast, if you are lucky enough to be in a movie which is shot largely on location you can have an absolutely wonderful time. In this respect I really did rather well. Of the modest number of movies that I made, five of them took me to parts of the world as diverse and fascinating as Israel, Mallorca, Yugoslavia, Southern Italy, and Nigeria. Even with the most efficient and well-organised Location Manager and First Assistant Director there are bound to be lots of days when you are not working or on call, which means plenty of leisure time to explore the region, go sightseeing and get to know the people.

The film *Masada* was mostly shot around the shores of the Dead Sea and the surrounding desert, and some of it actually on the great rock of Masada itself. This was where Herod built his summer palace, but it was also the fortress where the Jews made their last stand against the Romans. The great revolt against Roman occupation had begun in AD66, and by AD72 Masada was the last remaining stronghold of resistance. The Romans besieged the fortress, and for an entire year a community of Jewish Zealots, numbering nine hundred and sixty men, women and children, held at bay the whole Tenth Legion plus a small army of auxiliaries. The Zealots were well prepared with stocks of food, and huge cisterns cut into the rock held a plentiful supply of water, topped up by ingenious aqueducts to catch the flood water which occasionally swept by. Finally the Romans brought in siege machinery and broke into the fortress, to find that the Zealots had burned all their possessions and taken their own lives, preferring to die free rather than live in slavery.

It was intensely moving to stand on the top of that great rock and look down to see, far below, the red tents of the Tenth Legion which our set designers had erected in the sand at the foot of the slope. This artificial show of theatricality in such a haunted place should have seemed like a brash, unfeeling intrusion, but somehow it did not. For me, at least, it gave the most vivid sense of what it must have been like, almost two thousand years ago, to wake each morning and see that sprawling red encampment still down there, still implacably waiting, and think to yourself 'How long?' Then, as I walked round and saw the remains of small stone fireplaces and little baby-sized seats cut into the rock, I could envisage the day when you knew that at last the waiting was over. The last family meal had been cooked over that little fireplace, your possessions were all burnt, and you killed your children, you killed your wife and, before the first Roman soldier reached the plateau, you killed yourself. Absurdly, wearing as I was the uniform of a Roman Commander, I almost felt the terrible weight of guilt myself.

No such dark imaginings overshadowed the pure, sunlit joy of six blissful weeks in Mallorca shooting *Evil under the Sun*. An Agatha Christie story (as, of course, was *Murder on the Orient Express*), this one had for its Hercule Poirot the lovely Peter Ustinov, surely the wittiest, warmest, most charming companion one could dare wish for, both as a working colleague and as a friend to unwind with off-duty. Better still, Diana Rigg and I were back together (married again, of course); I was working with James Mason for the first time, having washed up his breakfast at the Dorchester all those years ago, and to top it all the ineffable Maggie Smith was on hand with her inimitable drawl and her acerbic quips about all and sundry.

The only fly in the ointment was the director. A well-established film-maker with a track record as long as your arm – mostly action movies, all expertly done – Guy Hamilton was, like Sidney Lumet, completely at home in all the technical aspects of the job. Unlike Lumet, however, he seemed to think that directing the actors was none of his business. On my first day in Mallorca I spent some time watching a scene being run through just prior to shooting. Not a lot seemed to be happening. As I had a couple of alternative ideas about the interpretation of my character, I asked the First Assistant Director (he's the man who really keeps things running on a film-set) whether he thought I might be able to grab a few minutes sometime for a quick chat with Mr Hamilton before I immortalised anything on film the following day. He drew me aside and with a reassuring smile said:

'I think you'll find, Sir, that Guy has surrounded himself with a group of fine actors whose work he admires, so if you don't hear anything, you can assume that everything is all right.'

This was a polite way of saying: 'Don't expect any direction whatever, mate,' and he was very soon proved right. The first time I asked a question, the reply was: 'Hm-hm. Excuse me. Hm-hm,' and Guy went and adjusted a lamp. After this had happened a few times, Peter Ustinov drew a big cartoon of Guy and me, with a huge balloon coming out of my mouth, saying:

'Guy, I've just discovered that lady killed my wife. Shall I jump up and try to hit her, or sit and bury my face in my hands, or what do you think?' And the balloon coming out of Guy's mouth said:

'Hm-hm, with a bit of luck, Denis, hm-hm, you won't be in the shot.'

On James Mason's first shooting day he came and sat next to me in the lunch tent looking distraught.

'What's the matter, James?'

'I'm not being allowed to play my part.'

James was playing a brash American theatre producer, and being a very fine character actor, he had come up with a splendidly vulgar creation. After the first walk-through on the set, Guy had said to him:

'James, your public loves you for your handsome appearance and your beautiful voice – just be yourself, old boy, just be yourself.'

James found a compromise which worked well enough, but I would love to have seen his original idea come to life on the screen.

If you think that Mallorca is all high-rise concrete blocks filled with shaven-headed, tattooed hooligans drinking Double Diamond in discos and chanting 'Engerland, Engerland,' let me reassure you. You may well encounter this on one small stretch of the south coast, but the whole of the north-west – and indeed most of the island – is ravishingly beautiful and very largely unspoilt. The coast road from Andraitx up to Formentor is breathtaking – at least the equal of the much more famous Amalfi Drive.

I was swimming one day in the warm, clear sea somewhere near Deya when Ken Lintott, who had created a splendidly ugly distorted skull for me when I played Caliban in *The Tempest*, and was now doing a rather simpler job as my make-up man in *Evil under the Sun*, swam gently towards me:

'Denis.'

'Yes, Ken?'

'I think this location is my reward for enduring three months in Jutland filming *King Lear* with Peter Brook.'

Lazily and happily we swam back together for lunch.

The next morning I came down to the hotel lobby as usual to be driven to the location, and was told that I had a new driver that day, as the regular one was sick. 'It's the brown Mercedes over there,' said the transport manager. As I walked towards the brown Mercedes a mellifluous Spanish voice cried gaily from the driver's seat:

'Ah – buenas dias Señor Queelay, I am Pedro, very, very good driver, I take you wherever you wish to go. Vamos!'

It was Peter Ustinov, of course, doing one of his turns. There was nothing wrong with my driver – Peter had just decided he would like to drive me, and he kept up the Pedro character all the way. As we passed through Valdemosa: 'Here was living famous composer Frederico Chopping, with French lady always wearing trousers. Very,

very strange.' We arrived at the location in a relaxed and ebullient mood which lasted all day, as it usually did whenever Peter was around.

To make things even better, all the family – Stella, Sarah, Joanna and David – came out to join me for two whole weeks. I was only working for two or three odd days during those weeks, so we had all the time in the world to swim, sunbathe and discover the beauties of the island and courtesy of the people. Just a handsomely paid holiday, really.

Another big bonus was the trip to New York to do the publicity for the film's American release. Half a dozen of us were flown out with our wives, boyfriends, etc, and put up in the St Regis Hotel, which has just the '20s/'30s feel of the movie itself. We spent three beautifully organised days talking to the press, the radio stations and all the TV networks, and then on the last evening there was to be a dinner party. We were to be split up, with one of us at each table to keep the media people and PR people happy. This, I thought to myself, is going to be a really hard evening's work. It turned out to be an absolute gas. The media people were all unbuttoned and convivial now that they had done their work, and seemed genuinely to have enjoyed the movie. Better than that, though, Celeste Holm was at my table, chatting with me like an old chum, Ethel Merman was at the next-door table, and several other stars were dotted around the room. Dinner passed in a flash.

We had been told that there would be some after-dinner entertainment, but had no idea what form it would take. I was open-mouthed with disbelief and trying hard not to swoon in ecstasy when onto the stage, one by one, came four legendary veterans of Tin Pan Alley and Hollywood: Sammy Cahn, ace lyric-writer and raconteur; Arthur Schwartz, the surviving member of the Dietz and Schwartz songwriting team; Charles Strouse, composer of *Annie*; and best of all (and oldest!) Herb Green, who was Fred Astaire's pianist and Musical Director.

All the incidental music in our movie, including 'You're the Top' which Diana Rigg sang with me at the piano, was by Cole Porter, so he was the composer of the evening. Each of these old guys came on in turn, sat at the piano and sang a couple of Cole Porter numbers. The voices were not what they had been (if indeed they ever were) but they knew everything there is to know about how to put a number over. As they were leaving the stage to wild applause at the end of their act, Sammy Cahn called them all back, saying: 'Hold on there, fellers, one more number,' and handed out sheets of paper; he had written a new lyric to 'You're the Top,' full of in-jokes about the four of them, and about *Evil under the Sun*. After a bit of 'Goddammit, I can't find my glasses' and much shuffling of song-sheets, they all launched into it with gusto, brought the house down and finally escaped.

Just as I was thinking it was all over, and life didn't get any better than this, Herb Green reappeared, went to the table next to mine and whispered in Ethel Merman's ear. After a few seconds of unconvincing mock-reluctance she cried, 'Oh well – OK, OK,' and strode up onto the stage. 'E-flat, one verse, one chorus,' she instructed Mr Green, and the Grande Dame burst into song – 'My story is much too sad to be to-o-old' – and we were treated to the Merman version of 'I get a Kick out of You'. The voice was still like a trumpet, and the 'after-dinner entertainment' had surpassed the wildest expectations.

Soon after we got back to London, Bernard, my agent, rang to say: 'I've been sent the script of a film which is going to be shot in Yugoslavia. Peter Ustinov is directing and playing one of the leads, and he would like you to be in it.'

'I'll do it.'

'Hold on – you haven't read it yet. It's not a very good part, and…'

'If it's with Peter, I'll do it.'

In the event it wasn't a bad little part. The film was called *Memed my Hawk* and the shoot was predictably enjoyable, even one scene which started off rather unpromisingly. Michael Elphick and I were required to deliver dialogue containing crucial plot lines, plus the occasional jest, while wading shoulder high through a cold, dirty and smelly lake. The weather was grey and depressing, and after a few abortive takes and restarts everyone was getting a bit tetchy. This was a cue for song which I could not resist. 'There's a bright golden haze on the meadow,' I carolled, with a cheerful grin pasted onto my frozen face; Peter joined in round about 'the corn is as high as an elephant's eye,' Mike Elphick tentatively croaked along with 'and it looks like it's climbin' clear up to the sky,' and the whole crew chorused, 'Oh what a beautiful mornin',' right through to the end. We got the scene in the next take.

Two years later Peter was a guest on my *This is your Life*, and when Eammon Andrews asked him, 'And have you ever heard Denis sing, Peter?' he replied: 'Yes, frequently – usually when he was up to his neck in freezing water.' Diana Rigg was another of the guests, and the BBC had sent a camera over specially to New York to record a contribution from dear old Harry Watkins, my dresser from *Irma la Douce*, who was now in his 90s and too frail to make the journey to London. He delivered a touching little tribute which had the whole studio in tears, and ended by saying, with his beautiful ear-to-ear smile: '… and Mr Quilley, I never thought I'd be on the same TV show as Miss Diana Rigg!'

We filmed *Memed* in Zagreb, a grey, forbidding city, populated by the most unforbidding and hospitable people, and in Skopje, down south in Macedonia. Here, if it weren't for the Cyrillic script on all the shop fronts and public buildings, one could almost imagine oneself to be in Italy – warm sunshine, pavement cafés in small squares with fountains, and people radiating an outgoing Mediterranean warmth.

On one of my strolls around the town I tripped over a paving-stone and ripped most of the sole off my shoe. My command of Serbo-Croat extended no further than 'Cheers,' 'Goodnight' and 'Thank you,' but a vigorous leg-waving dumb-show brought laughs and smiles from several passers-by, who all pointed to the same spot just down the street, and there, indeed, was a shoe-repair shop. Inside, the cobbler was at his last, cutting leather and banging nails. I dangled my shoe in the air with a hopeful look on my face. 'OK,' he said, and took it from me, pointing me to a chair. As I sat, he put aside the work he was doing and started straight away on my shoe. He shouted something to the back of the shop, and in a moment a young boy appeared (his son, I gathered) carrying a cup of tea which he pressed solemnly into my hand. I drank it gratefully while I watched his father deftly putting my shoe back together. When he had finished, I thanked him and took out some money to pay him. He waved it away firmly, saying, 'No, no.' I tried to insist, but he was adamant. 'No, no. Friend, Friend, OK?' I shook his hand and said: 'Yes, OK. Friend, *Friend*!'

A little of this bonhomie would have gone down a treat in Nigeria, where a movie called *Mister Johnson* took me next. Chief Ogunde, in whose territory we were shooting, was helping us by supplying a lot of extras, one camera and crew from his own film company, and crucial local knowledge and contacts. He had also supplied me with a letter stating that I was working for him and should be given every assistance, etc, etc. As I soon discovered, this was basically to ensure that I didn't get shot.

I was met at Kano airport by a sweet, giggly little lady who informed me that she was one of Chief Ogunde's wives, and was here to escort me through all the formalities so that there would not be any problems. As we approached the entrance to the airport building a very large soldier, aged about eighteen at a guess, wearing camouflage battledress with a Kalashnikov slung on his shoulder, stopped my little lady with a big upraised hand and barked aggressively:

'Where is your pass?'

She giggled a little and told him that she was only here to accompany me, but didn't quite get around to telling him who she was. (He didn't seem to care who I was.) Suddenly the Kalashnikov was off his shoulder and pointing at her.

'I said where is your fucking PASS?'

My little lady was not giggling now; her problem-solving mission had met with an early setback. Inspiration descended upon me: I reached into my pocket, took out my laissez-passer letter and held it up in front of him.

'This is from Chief Ogunde.'

His head whipped round as though stung by a bee.

'Ogunde?'

He glanced at the letter, though I don't think he could read, and repeated: 'Ogunde, OK.'

He opened the door, stepped back and waved us in. Round one to me; round two coming up – Passport Control. Nigeria was a military dictatorship at the time, and a big picture of the colonel in charge of this district hung on the wall behind four men who sat in a row on a dais raised just high enough to be slightly intimidating.

'Do I choose one of them?' I whispered to my little friend.

'No,' she giggled (her confidence had returned and with it the giggle). 'No – you have to go through all four of them.'

I handed my passport to number one, who spent five minutes studying the photograph and comparing it with my face before deciding that we were probably one and the same person. Number two studied every visa and entry and exit stamp, and conceded that I might, indeed, have come from London, as I claimed. I am not quite sure what number three's function was, but it entailed a lot of whispering in number two's ear and doubtful glances in my direction. Number four wasted no time at all. He opened the passport at the front page and instantly thrust it at my face, shouting: 'Who is that?'

(It was a photograph of my son, who was now about twenty, but was perhaps nine or ten when the picture was taken, so that he could travel with me without having a separate passport of his own – a common practice.)

'That's my son.'

'Where is he?' he shouted loudly.

'In Australia.'

'Why is he not here?' (Even louder.)

'Er, well, basically because he's back-packing round Australia.'

It would all have been rather funny except that two more large young men with Kalashnikovs, attracted by the shouting, were now standing on either side of me, and I got the distinct feeling that if I was too rude to this man or said the wrong thing I would never be seen again. My little lady had reverted to silent non-giggle mode, so – out came the Ogunde letter once again, and once again it worked its magic, and in no time we were in the unit hotel, where a young pre-Bond Pierce Brosnan was trying in vain to get a decent bottle of wine to go with his dinner. It seemed he had been trying ever since he arrived, several days before me, and he certainly went on trying all the time I was there with no success. By this time I was not fussy, and happily shared with him a bottle of quite drinkable plonk. Pierce proved to be very good company, and with the genial and talented Aussie director Bruce Beresford in charge everything went smoothly.

The big problem was the telephone. On a film location the people in the office are on the phone to London or LA the whole time, to the producers, to the actors' agents and so on. The little difficulty here was that it took about four hours to get through to London, which meant that with luck you might manage to make two or three calls in a day. Eventually someone discovered a sort of post-office-cum-telephone exchange just down the road from the hotel where you could get through in half an hour. There were four phone booths at one end of the room with no doors, so all the assembled locals could hear everything you said, and the lines were so bad that you had to shout to make yourself heard.

'I said I LOVE YOU!' I shouted one day – the local ladies queuing behind me found this very touching.

'I love you too,' Stella's voice shouted at the other end, 'but I have some very bad news for you. Gordon has died.'

'Gordon?' I yelled, in shock, 'Gordon *Jackson?*'

Yes, Gordon was dead – he had come to dinner in our house only weeks before. I burst into tears, mumbled goodbyes and stumbled out through all those waiting ladies, who were now trying to console me.

'Hey Mister,' called the man behind the pay desk.

Oh God, I must have gone over my time (I had paid in advance as instructed).

'I suppose I owe you money?' I said wearily.

'No, Mister, you were under time – I owe *you* money.'

This simple act of generosity set me crying again. I took the money, thanked everybody, pulled myself together and walked sadly up the hill to the hotel.

Suddenly I couldn't wait to get home.

Chapter 11
Exits and Entrances

WHEN JOHN NEVILLE came back to London to play Sir Peter Teazle in *The School for Scandal* after spending some twenty years in Canada running the theatre in Stratford, Ontario, he arrived at the National Theatre for the first rehearsal white-faced with shock. When we asked him what was wrong, he stammered:

'I've never seen scenes like that anywhere outside India!'

What on earth was he talking about? Well, it seems he walked from Waterloo Station to the National via the under pass below the big Waterloo roundabout. A perfectly sensible route to take, except that the entire area under the roundabout (and it is a huge area) was filled to bursting with people living in cardboard boxes, or sleeping-bags, or just a blanket on a ground-sheet. Sadly we had to tell him that although he had certainly stumbled upon an extreme example, this was now a commonplace sight all over large stretches of this great city, including the West End.

This was 1990; it had built up gradually over the years and we had got used to it, and as I write this a dozen years on, nothing has changed. On my short walk from the Embankment over Hungerford Bridge and along the river to the National I am regularly asked for 'spare change' by half-a-dozen or more youngsters – and this is the thing: they are all youngsters, teens and twenties, whose lives are already blighted and desolate. They are not all drug addicts; they are certainly not all con-artists, as some people uncharitably suggest – surely nobody would spend all day sitting by the roadside hunched up under a blanket in every kind of weather except as a last resort; and they can't all be escaping from families so ghastly that anything is preferable to living with Mum and Dad. I stop to talk to them sometimes, and although they are quite forthcoming about what their daily routine is (stay here until they've collected enough for something to eat and drink, then come back until there's enough for some sort of shelter for the night) it is very difficult to get them to explain how and why they come to be living like this. These are mostly intelligent and able-bodied kids who should either be living at home or getting some kind of job. There *are* jobs if you're not too fussy, and surely even menial ones like cleaning, serving Big Macs or washing-up (yes – I'm showing off) are better than freezing on the streets for small change. Of course, one always used to see the occasional tramp or wino looking for hand-outs, but they were old fellows who had been through a bit of life and given up; it is the extreme youth of these boys and girls which is new and disturbing. I can't explain it, and I don't know anyone who can. It saddens me and baffles me.

However, John Neville soon cheered up when he saw what an inventive and refreshing production *The School for Scandal* was going to be. My daughter Joanna was a scenic artist at the National at the time, and she was astonished one day to be given the job of painting an enormous sailing ship. She came home from work that night and said:

'Dad – what's a sailing ship doing in *The School for Scandal*?'

A good question – every scene of the play takes place in a room in someone's house. But she had reckoned without the dynamic director, Peter Wood. I was playing Uncle Oliver, who returns from Eastern parts halfway through the play. The stage direction says: 'A room in Sir Peter Teazle's house. Enter Sir Oliver Surface.' Peter Wood had other ideas. John Neville as Sir Peter entered onto a quayside and looked expectantly offstage. Round went the revolving stage, and on came a stately ship in full sail, with pennants flying. It stopped at the quayside, and down the gang-plank, preceded by a little Oriental boy carrying a lot of luggage, came a resplendent figure in eighteenth century tropical whites, with a straw tricorn hat on his head and a fly-whisk in his hand. Yes, reader, it was I. Uncle Oliver had never had such a splendid entrance before, and I venture to predict never will again.

A couple of years later, Peter pulled off a similar *coup de théatre* at Chichester, another big open stage which, like the Olivier, is ideally suited to this kind of big, bold staging. The opening of *She Stoops to Conquer* reads: 'A chamber in an old-fashioned house. Enter Mrs Hardcastle and Mr Hardcastle,' but the loyal patrons of the Chichester Festival were treated to an opening which was much more fun. I, as Mr Hardcastle, strode out onto an empty stage carrying a double-barrelled shot-gun and surrounded by a crowd of marksmen and servants; we all looked up to the sky, and – 'Aha!' – I raised my shotgun and fired, and a handsome, plump pheasant dropped like a stone from the sky into the welcoming arms of one of my servants. The audience loved it, and when the play proper began, they were already in a happy and expectant mood before a line was spoken.

Between these two plays, filled with the warm-hearted wit and wisdom of Sheridan and Goldsmith, we ventured into the very different, very murky world of John Webster and *The White Devil*. This play, and Webster's other major piece (probably his masterpiece) *The Duchess of Malfi*, are much performed and much admired by the *cognoscenti*, but I find it impossible to enjoy his work. He writes beautifully, of course, and there is a huge intelligence and imaginative energy in his whole body of work, but the heart in that body seems to me to be rotten. There is a self-indulgent, lip-smacking enjoyment of the violence that he describes so poetically, and a deep vein of misogyny runs through it all. I have the feeling that consciously or subconsciously he blamed women for the syphilis which was increasing its hold in England about this time (the early seventeenth century).

So here I was playing Brachiano, a role for which I was twenty years too old, in a play that I heartily disliked, but at least it gave me the opportunity to play opposite the beautiful black actress Josette Simon, even if she was young enough to be my daughter. Near the end of the play, Flamineo, in a typically cruel Webster joke, raises a pistol and aims it point-blank at the girl's head. As the poor child moans in terror he pulls the trigger – click! And with a hateful smile he says: 'There were no bullets in the gun.' One night the actor playing Flamineo picked up, or was given, the wrong gun as he came on stage, one which instead of being empty was loaded with blanks intended to be fired in another scene. An awful lot of junk comes out when a blank is fired; not only the hot blast of the explosion, but hot gunpowder, sometimes little bits of cartridge-case, and if it is anywhere near your face it can be extremely painful and extremely dangerous. In this case it was about six inches from Josette's face, and all that stuff hit her smack in the eye.

I was in my dressing room, but over the PA system I heard the shot, a scream, and then a deathly silence. Josette had run off, sobbing and shaking, but somehow, incredibly, managed to hold herself together and went back on to finish the show. The audience, who realised all too clearly what had happened, gave her an ovation, then she was whizzed off to hospital, where they found serious damage to the cornea and crossed their fingers that the retina was unharmed. It was; the cornea healed, and Josette came back to work – too soon, as it transpired. When the stage manager's voice on the tannoy called, 'Half an hour, please,' she started to shake uncontrollably from head to foot and could hardly speak. She was taken straight home, and stayed there until the emotional wounds had mended as well as the physical, and then finally managed to get back on stage and put herself through it again. I felt like looking up (no, more likely *down*) to where Webster sat and watched all this, and saying: 'You see, John – this is what happens when you play cruel sadistic mind-games with people.' Stupid, really; he didn't switch the guns – though he might have done if he'd thought of it.

There are those who are as disturbed by the violence in *Sweeney Todd* as I am by *The White Devil* and *The Duchess of Malfi*, but there is an enormous, basic difference, a difference in kind. Sweeney is a man raging against a world which has savagely mistreated him, and against one man in particular. He was deported to Australia on a trumped-up charge, and the judge who falsely and deliberately convicted him has seduced and stolen his wife, who is now reduced to a crazed beggar-woman. His daughter, now a grown-up young woman, is the legal ward of that same judge, who secretly lusts after her as well. Sweeney is implacable in his desire for revenge, which he finally achieves in the bloodiest way possible. But there is no gratuitous violence, none of Webster's unhealthy relish. And the man has suffered so much that it is easy to sympathise with him, unlike Webster's protagonist who seems to enjoy cruelty for its own sake.

I was reminded of all this when, after a rejuvenating and refreshing season at Chichester playing *Venus Observed* and *She Stoops to Conquer* (a palate-cleansing sorbet after Webster's over-ripe dish of game), I bumped into Stephen Sondheim in the West End. We had a drink together, and talked of this and that, and then he said:

'Did you know they're doing *Sweeney Todd* at the National?'

'Yes, but they are going for Alun Armstrong as Sweeney. He's younger than me, and very different, and he'll be very good.'

'Well, that's OK – you're twelve years older now – why don't you play the Judge?'

'I would love to, but only if they put back the flagellation scene.'

'O-oh, you'll be lucky – I wouldn't bet on it.'

What we were talking about was an absolutely marvellous number, almost operatic in its intensity, which is actually in the original Broadway cast recording, but was cut from the show by Hal Prince after the first preview, and never performed in any production thereafter, including ours at Drury Lane. The Judge, stripped to the waist, is spying on Johanna through the keyhole of her room, singing of how desperately he desires her while punishing himself with a whip and calling on God for forgiveness: 'Mea culpa, mea culpa, mea maxima, maxima culpa!' It is a riveting portrayal of a man who is outwardly the very soul of integrity and respectability, but inwardly racked by repressed sexuality and religious guilt. It comes out of nowhere as a complete surprise, and is deeply disturbing and revealing. It shows the judge as a driven, flawed and complex character, and without it and the scene which evolves from it he is just a two-dimensional baddie, much less interesting, and much less challenging to play.

I was, and I remain, mystified as to why Hal wanted to cut it, and even more mystified that Stephen allowed him to. I can only imagine that as Hal had successfully directed many of his previous shows, Stephen regarded him as a lucky talisman, or as a guru who must know best. Fortunately, when the National asked me to play the Judge, and I said: 'Only if we put back the flagellation scene,' the Musical Director Mark Dorrell, a superb musician who knows a great piece of music when he hears it, instantly said 'Of course, we *must* have it back – I can't imagine why it was ever cut!' We were off to a good start.

This production of *Sweeney* was directed by Declan Donnellan, and was as different from the one we did with Hal Prince in 1980 as could possible be imagined. Instead of the two thousand seats and enormous stage of Drury Lane we had the three hundred seats and intimate little playing area of the Cottesloe, the smallest and most friendly of the three National auditoria. Instead of an orchestra of about thirty in the pit we had a chamber ensemble of nine sitting up on two shelves on either side of us, and instead of a chorus of about twenty we had no chorus at all. The choruses were all sung by the company of actors who, as well as playing their own parts, stayed on stage throughout, watching the action, silently commenting on it, and sometimes taking an active part in it – one of the men, for example, handed me the whip for the flagellation scene.

This was a staging concept which Declan had brought to perfection over the years while working with his touring company Cheek by Jowl, and like all the other changes it worked like a dream. The small space brought the audience into absolutely face-to-face contact with the action; the much smaller orchestral and choral forces more than made up for the loss of weight and volume with infinitely greater clarity, both of instrumental lines and of verbal subtleties. The best change of all, which one might have feared would be a great loss but turned out to be a great gain, was the drastic simplification of the stage scenery. The huge Drury Lane stage was filled with great Victorian structures, including that aforementioned bridge on which I smashed my head on the opening night; machinery of all kinds filled every space and spilled out round the proscenium arch. It was wonderfully evocative and impressive, but in fact it was all, as far as the actual drama was concerned, strictly unnecessary. All the crucial action took place centre stage in a small, simple movable truck housing Mrs Lovett's pie-shop on the ground floor and Mr Todd's

Tonsorial Parlour above it. And that, basically, was what our set at the National consisted of.

This intense concentration of the action in such a small space had an electrifying impact on the audience. I could clearly see them leaning forward spellbound by the beauty of some of the arias, or turning away in horror at the gorier moments – Larry Olivier would have *loved* it, despite his protestations about not wanting to see the faces 'out there'. Julia McKenzie was the definitive Mrs Lovett, combining the blowsy, slatternly charm of Angela Lansbury, who played it on Broadway with Sheila Hancock's lovable Cockney Sparrer perkiness, adding her own earthy sense of humour and most of all, of course, her magnificent singing voice. Singing a duet with Julia was like being picked up and carried.

The show was so successful that the little theatre couldn't possibly accommodate everyone who wanted to see it, and with other shows queuing up for the Cottesloe, Richard Eyre (the new Director of the National) proposed moving it to the Lyttleton. Alun Armstrong was having trouble with his voice, and didn't think he could manage any more, so Richard asked me if I would take over and revert to being Sweeney again. This was a tricky decision. Obviously I was dying for another go at the Barber, but, 'It won't go so well in that big cold space,' I said, cravenly, 'and I will get the blame.' 'I bet you it will,' said Richard, with an amused grin. He was right: it did, and I moved back home into my dear old Tonsorial Parlour with my wicked razors for company, happy as a sand-boy. And if I was happy, Stephen was ecstatic. No black depressions now, just huge smiles every time he came backstage after a performance – I had never seen him so happy.

We took the show to Cardiff, Newcastle, Budapest, Madrid and Bath, to great acclaim everywhere. As we took the curtain-call after the first night in Budapest, the whole of the stalls started clapping very, very slowly.

'Oh, my God,' whispered Julia in my ear, 'they're giving us the slow handclap.'

'Wait,' I whispered back. 'Wait.'

Very gradually the clapping got faster and faster until it erupted into cheers, foot-stamping and whistles, which all went on for quite a while. Julia's anxious face was transformed – she was suddenly a little girl floating on Hungarian Cloud Nine.

When the RSC asked me to play Terri Dennis in *Privates on Parade* all those years ago, their London home was in Aldwych, a lovely Edwardian theatre, all charm and friendly, welcoming curves. When they asked me to play Baron Von Epp in John Osborne's *A Patriot for Me* (another drag queen – does the RSC know something about me that nobody else does?), the ambience was not quite so user-friendly.

You may remember my helpful warnings about the difficulties you might experience arriving at the National Theatre for the first time as a would-be member of the audience and trying to find a way in without being mown down by a juggernaut. Well, at the Barbican Centre the RSC took this as a starting-point and refined it into something even more subtle and amusing. Your walk from the Barbican underground station is quite fun – it's a sort of paper-chase, with different coloured lines painted on the ground to lead you through the various parts of this vast, bleak, housing estate. Keep your head clear and your eyes down, Follow the Yellow Brick Road, and there is your destination ahead of you. At least you assume it is because, as at the National, the only door (the *only* door) which identifies itself in any way bears the legend 'Stage Door,' which means that the big square block over there on the other side must be the

Barbican Centre, housing the theatre, concert hall, cinema and other attendant delights. So that's where you head for.

Unfortunately there seems to be no way in. You case the joint from all angles, but no, there's no way in. The one thing that is absolutely crystal clear is that the way in couldn't *possibly* be down that ramp between the stage door and the Big Square Block down which is pouring a constant stream of cars and taxis heading, presumably, for an underground car park. You enquire at the Stage Door for directions, and they tell you that the way in is down that ramp where all the cars are going towards an underground car park. Overcoming your disbelief you walk, terrified, down the ramp, hugging the wall and waving the little red flag you always carry for just such an emergency as this, and at the bottom there are two large and impressive sets of glass doors, one ahead of you and one behind you. Some perverse logic tells you that the one behind you is the more likely of the two, and so it proves. You go through those doors and you are in. In a space the size of two generous aircraft hangars. Your ticket informs you that the entertainment of your choice is on (let's say) Level 4. Which level are you on now? Is Level 4 up or down from there? You ask a person who seems to work there, you find your Level eventually, of course, and when you get where you want to be you probably enjoy your evening very much. The work on offer is usually first rate, the concert hall is quite pleasant, and so is the theatre auditorium, apart from the myriad doors in the side walls which, just before the curtain rises, all close simultaneously and automatically with a concerted 'Whoosh' sending the unnervingly claustrophobic message: 'Now try to get out of here if you *dare*!'

If, like me, you are a worker rather than a spectator in this strange place you enter, of course, through that uniquely well signposted stage door. From this point on everything, *everything* is underground:

the dressing rooms, the canteen and green room, wardrobe, rehearsal rooms – everything. No daylight, no fresh air; you are entombed. There is a slight, apparent exception: as I was in the top echelon of the cast list I was privileged to have a dressing room with a window. The room was actually underground like everything else, and the window was a very small one, perhaps two feet square, but still, it was a window. It had been built to be openable, but very early in its short sad life had been hermetically sealed, and with good reason. Although quite a long way below street level, a glimmer of light did penetrate to the interior, but if you wanted some air to go with that glimmer, you would have opened the window to find that you were halfway down that ramp (yes, *that* ramp) and all those cars and taxis heading for the Underworld were six inches away from your nose. Claustrophobia would have seemed a marginally more attractive option than ear damage and carbon monoxide poisoning.

Do not let your brain confuse the two words 'Barbican' and 'Barbados'. Admittedly they begin with the same combination of letters, but then so do the two words 'Heaven' and 'Hell,' and Barbados for us is a kind of Heaven. It was there, thank God, that we were headed for next. It may not be as physically beautiful as St Lucia or as sophisticated as Jamaica, or have as many beaches as Antigua, but we love it.

On our first visit to Barbados we stayed at Cobblers Cove, an enchanting little collection of cottages up in the north of the island. One morning we awoke to see a US Coastguard vessel moored about half a mile off-shore – it had evidently arrived overnight. This was during Ronald Reagan's presidency, and I dimly remembered reading that he was visiting several Caribbean heads of state and also (rather more enjoyably for him, I imagine) calling on his old friend Claudette

Colbert, who had a house just along the beach from where we were staying. In the middle of the morning I was out sailing in one of those little one-man one-sail baby yachts which are so easy to handle that even I can sail them, when suddenly a rubber inflatable with two men aboard roared towards me from the Coastguard ship. One of the men stood up, raised a megaphone to his lips and shouted:

'Get back to shore, this is a restricted area. Repeat Restricted Area, get back to shore!'

I did as I was told – I didn't want to be clapped in irons. When I reached shore I found that the beach had been completely cleared and everyone was congregated in our garden, which overlooked the stretch of beach in front of Mme Colbert's house, and which we were now sharing with four TV cameras from the various American networks, plus every black security guard who could be mustered, all dressed up to look like Barbadian beach boys – not very successfully, especially as they all had walkie-talkies which were continuously squawking 'Mr President is about to do this' or Mr President has just done the other'.

Finally, Mr President did what they were all waiting for. The gate of the Colbert residence opened, and out bounded Ronnie, looking very trim in his elegant swim-shorts. He turned and waved towards where he had been told the TV cameras were (in our garden!) then strode manfully down the beach and plunged athletically into the sea. As soon as he was in, and the cameras had stopped rolling, *four* security men, also in swim shorts, trotted out of the gate and after him into the water. Were they carrying waterproof hand-guns in the pockets of their shorts, or did they perhaps have deadly shark-knives strapped to their thighs like Ursula Andress in *Dr No*? The world will never know. They caught up with Mr President, and the four of them formed a perfect square round him with the boss in the centre, and all five swam out in perfect symmetry, then turned round without breaking formation and swam back to shore. It was *exactly* like that wonderfully kitsch Synchronised Swimming that glamorous girls used to do in the Olympics. I kept waiting for them to roll over on their backs and flex their legs in the air to the tune of 'The Blue Danube,' but it was not to be; they disappeared back through the gate to have lunch with Claudette, and Stella's well-trained actress's voice rang out:

'Can our children go back onto the beach now, please?'

Nowadays we always stay within strolling distance of Holetown, a little township half-way up the West coast in the parish of St James. The Eastern, Atlantic side of the island is spectacularly beautiful but wild and dangerous for swimming, whereas the Western, Caribbean coast, with sandy beaches and a much warmer sea, is altogether lazier and more sybaritic. Holetown, though tiny, has a very decent little shopping centre, and several excellent restaurants and bars, and unlike Sandy Lane (of which more anon) is inhabited by real people. Respectable mothers and grandmothers in print dresses and straw hats on their way to church, Bible and Prayer-book in their white-gloved hands; little children on their way to school, the boys in immaculately pressed shirts and shorts, the girls in neat gym-slips and Persil-white blouses; young men on the beach bringing home fish caught that morning.

I always swim first thing every morning as soon as the sun is over the palm trees and onto the beach, before any of the other visitors are out of their beds. Just me and the sea wishing each other a nice day, and the occasional passing beach-boy for company. Over the years, they have always called a friendly greeting: 'Hey man, how ya doin'?' On our last trip, however, I was just a little taken aback when for the first time one of them cried: 'Hey! A'right, Daddy!' Oh lord, I thought, time is passing. Daddy! If only they knew, they would be calling 'A'right, Grandaddy!' But I won't enlighten them – they'll get around to that all too soon without any prompting from me. This was made quite clear to me a few evenings later when we had been out for dinner to a lovely little local restaurant perched on the rocks about six feet above the sea. We were in the foyer waiting for the boss to add up our bill, and as there was a rather nice smoochy Glenn Miller-ish dance number playing quietly on the muzak, Stella and I took a gentle little foxtrot round the room. Our host looked up from his mental arithmetic and with a big smile said:

'Oh – it's nice to see an elderly couple enjoyin' themselves.'

With mock indignation, and without breaking step, I replied:

'Not so much of the elderly please, if you don't mind!'

Quick as a flash, and absolutely dead-pan, his wife played the tag-line:

'I bin tellin' him for months – he need a new pair of glasses.'

On one of my early morning swims I ventured carelessly onto a big rock which, as I soon discovered, housed a few thousand sea-urchins, who welcomed me into their charming sea-side home by crying 'Hello!' and gleefully shooting spines from all directions into my naked, defenceless feet. Hearing me yell, and seeing me waving a foot ineffectually in the air one of a pair of passing beach-boys shouted to the other: 'Hey – the Big Fella's landed in the urchins!'

After being momentarily flattered to be described as Big, I was disconcerted to see them both apparently running away for dear life. How I misjudged them. By the time I hit the beach one of them was back from the beach bar, where he had found a lemon which he proceeded to squeeze all over my throbbing feet. Then his friend sprinted up with a candle and matches, lit the candle and dripped the molten wax all over the same ravaged area. My pained reaction to the hot wax gave them a few laughs, and then they had five minutes of harmless fun pulling out all the spines. Miraculously, when they had finished, the poor old feet were as good as new and I was able to carry on swimming. I had received the Bajan Emergency Sea-Urchin Cure – I recommend it as a stimulating start to the day.

The other great thing about Holetown, and the beaches to the north and south of it, is that it is completely and blessedly 'celebrity-free'. Well, Ronnie Barker comes to the same suite in the same hotel at the same time every year, and Felicity Kendal always stays at another hotel just up the road, but they are not what I mean by 'celebrities' – they are *stars*, and they are real, live, lovely people. No – the ones I mean all go to Sandy Lane. Sandy Lane, as I am sure most of you know, is the biggest, most luxurious and most expensive hotel complex on the island, and it has recently been rebuilt to make it even bigger, more luxurious and more expensive. If you are a celeb or a wannabe celeb, that's the place to stay.

For us, this particular visit, beautifully timed as the perfect antidote to the rigours of the Barbican, was the happy result of an invitation from the Kidds. Johnny and Wendy Kidd, father and mother of supermodel Jodie, live in a beautiful, not grand, but elegant plantation house on top of Holders Hill with a big, bountiful garden looking over the polo ground and out to a splendid view of the sea. Every year in March they host a month-long festival, usually featuring a Shakespeare play, an opera and a musical. This year they were giving *Twelfth Night*, in which I played Sir Toby Belch, Puccini's *Tosca*, and *HMS Pinafore* by Gilbert and Sullivan. The performances take place in the garden, the stage is a raised grassy knoll, the audience (six hundred of them) sit at tables on the lawn, there are coloured lights in the trees and fireflies flitting from branch to branch, the evening air is soft and balmy, and in all adds up to one of the most delightful experiences you can imagine. The audience is a mixture of locals and visitors, and the best audience of all are the local schoolchildren who are invited to the public dress rehearsals. They don't miss a trick. Children always love physical comedy of course, but these boys and girls get every verbal allusion in the Shakespeare play; veiled references to doubtful sexual identity are greeted with 'Oohs' and 'Aahs,' and Orsino's stunning first entrance, bareback on a horse, gets a well-deserved cheer. The whole festival is like a delectable mixture of Glyndebourne, a local village celebration, and the open-air Theatre in Regent's Park on an exceptionally warm evening.

Luckily for me, Regent's Park was exactly where my next job took me – the perfect soft landing back in London from Barbados. I had been there years before playing Benedick in *Much Ado*, but this was a different matter – Prospero in *The Tempest*. If there is a more perfect setting for this wonderful, magical play than Regent's Park, I can't think where it might be. At the end of the evening, after my final farewell to Ariel,

> ... my Ariel, chick,
> That is thy charge. Then to the elements
> Be free, and fare thou well

Ariel disappeared from his tree-top perch, and a soft light like a Barbadian firefly flew lightly from his branch to perch on the next tree, then to the next and on to the last, and then took off into the night sky and disappeared from view.

Impossible to follow? Not quite – the Old Vic beckoned once again. A quick, no-nonsense phone call from Peter Hall:

'Hello, chum – how would you like to play Gloucester in *King Lear*?'

'You're on!'

And off we went, back to the Waterloo Road.

Chapter 12
What's it all about, Alfie?

THAT SEASON which Peter Hall directed at the Old Vic in 1997 was everything that such a season should be. He chose exactly the right kind of repertoire for this theatre, so steeped in history but now looking to the future, thanks to the enthusiasm and extraordinary generosity of Toronto shopkeeper and theatre-lover Ed Mirvish, who, as well as backing the season, had made it financially possible for the rickety old building to be restored and tactfully modernised.

King Lear, *Waiting for Godot*, and *Waste* by Harley Granville-Barker – a Shakespeare masterpiece, a modern classic, and a little-known but perfectly crafted piece from 1907 by one of the theatre's great all-rounders. Three plays full of red meat into which any self-respecting actor would relish sinking his teeth. And that is just what we did – Alan Howard, Ben Kingsley, Greg Hicks and I, and a rock-solid company of eleven hand-picked by Peter, not for starriness but for talent and enthusiasm. It was a genuine repertory company – the same actors played in all three plays. The whole set-up was so perfect that it took me back to the halcyon days with Larry Olivier in the same building in the early '70s, in other words, my idea of theatrical heaven. Instead of Monday evenings we played 4pm matinées on Sundays. You may imagine the effect it had on us, on beautiful bright sunny afternoons (usually death at the Box Office) performing to packed houses of *young* people totally absorbed in these great works, amused and moved, and wildly enthusiastic at the end.

It was obvious that we had to do a second season (and perhaps a third, fourth and fifth?). Even Ed Mirvish's pockets were not bottomless, so Peter asked the Arts Council for £500,000 as a guarantee against loss – not a subsidy; if we broke even it would cost them nothing.

They turned him down.

We broke up after that one season, and that was the end of what could and should have been a triumphant return to the glory days of this grand old theatre. This is the same Arts Council who, when Tim Piggott-Smith took over Compass Theatre after Tony Quayle's death, surprised and delighted him by agreeing to give him three-year forward funding, thus enabling him to assure theatre managements in Belfast, Liverpool or wherever, that Compass would visit their city in the same month next year, the year after, and the year after that. This, in turn, would make it possible to start building a regular and loyal audience who would know what Compass was all about, for I promise you it is not easy to follow a sold-out week of *Russ Abbot's Roadshow* into a big variety house like the Sunderland Empire with a play called *The Royal Hunt of the Sun* (as we did) for an audience that has never heard of Compass Theatre and has no idea what the play is about – how would they without a bit of advance publicity? Tim, naturally, was overjoyed – this kind of forward funding was what he had always hoped for.

Next time I saw him he looked suicidal. The Arts Council had gone back on their promise, withdrawn the offer of three-year funding, and were now only prepared to give what they called Project Funding, which meant they would consider funding only one production at a time, and the choice of play had to be approved by their Drama Panel. Tim was devastated, but made up his mind to make the best of it – after all, even Project Funding was better than absolutely nothing at all. He decided he would mount a production of Chekhov's *The Seagull*. When he put the suggestion to the Drama Panel for their approval, one of its members said:

'*The Seagull*? What's that – is it a good play? Who wrote it?'

This from a member of the *Drama* Panel of the Arts Council of Great Britain and Northern Ireland. It is a wonder that any of the arts flourish at all in this country when such ignorant imposters hold the purse-strings.

But Tim still had one ace up his sleeve. Peter Shaffer, the author of *Royal Hunt*, had been so impressed by our production that he gave Tim the touring rights to *Amadeus*, his highly successful play about Mozart and Salieri. Tim's tour of *Amadeus* did so well that by the end of it Compass Theatre, for the very first time in its entire existence, went into profit. They were £27,000 in the black: not a vast amount but a triumph for Tim and a vindication of the whole idea behind the company's existence. The Arts Council responded to this magnificent achievement by saying that the entire £27,000 be returned to the Arts Council. (That same year they had spent £60,000 on relocating their London office.)

At this point, Tim, who until now had displayed saintly patience and heroic determination, finally threw up his hands in despair and gave up on the whole impossible situation. Compass Theatre was no more.

Another triumph for the Arts Council.

I always enjoy working in Chichester. It is a beautiful city, big enough to have all the amenities one could possibly need, but small enough to be comfortably walked from end to end or side to side. The traffic-free centre is a joy, with relaxed, strolling, window-shopping crowds proving daily what a pleasure civilised city-living can be. The beach at West Wittering is one of the best in England – a vast expanse of very gently sloping sand, wonderful for swimming, safe for children, and at low tide, when the sea retreats almost out of sight, a sensation of immense and liberating space, a lifting of the spirit that I also felt, unlikely though it may seem, in the totally different environment of Australia.

The Festival Theatre itself was an impossible, quixotic venture which has succeeded beyond everyone's wildest expectations. The brainchild of Leslie Evershed-Martin, a theatre-loving optician, it sits in parkland on the northern edge of the city. In a fine evening, you can sip your pre-show drinks at a table in the sun on the outdoor terrace looking over the park; if the weather is bad there is room for everyone in the spacious foyer. If you want to eat there are two restaurants, one posh and one self-service. For the main auditorium Evershed-Martin and his fellow gamblers crossed their fingers and went for broke: instead of a medium-sized, sedate, traditional theatre, they came up with a huge amphitheatre curving round the sides of the big thrust stage. In size and style it is very like the Olivier auditorium, so you can imagine it suits me very well. For smaller events there is the Minerva, which fulfils a similar function to the National's Cottesloe.

A word here in praise of the much-maligned Chichester audience. They are not by any means the stuffy and conventional bunch some critics would have you believe. Many of them may be mature in years, but they are also mature in judgment – they know quality when they see it, and respond to it warmly and enthusiastically. I have performed before them often, always with confidence and pleasure; on this particular occasion I was the Bishop of Southwark in *Racing Demon*, David Hare's fascinating and witty study of the Church of England, and in *Katherine Howard* by William Nicholson I was Wicked Uncle to the up-and-coming Emilia Fox. I enjoyed myself a lot. A season at the Chichester Festival is both literally and metaphorically a breath of fresh air.

215

Back home in Hampstead, at the New End Theatre, an intriguing piece called *Brief Candle*, an affectionate portrait of Marie Bashkirtsev by Carlo Ardito (London theatre critic for *Plays International* and principal translator of Eduardo de Filippo) gave me the challenge of playing half-a-dozen roles ranging from a callow young lover to an aged Pope, and the pleasure of being directed by Stella.

Having heroically given up a promising acting career many years before, to devote herself to bringing up three children, Stella eased herself back into the business by way of teaching and directing. She spent fifteen years teaching at the City Literary Institute (universally and affectionately known as the City Lit), an excellent adult education college just off Drury Lane, where she ran a Workshop for Musicals and directed a show every year. Among her distinguished alumni were Alistair Beaton, later the acclaimed author of *Feelgood*, and the wife of Charles Spencer, the Daily Telegraph theatre critic. 'Your wife taught my wife how to act!' he declared at our first meeting.

Stella also directed a series of productions at the Shaw Theatre, as a showcase for young actors working for an Equity card; she devises and directs recitals of poetry and music, sometimes with me, sometimes with others; she stages my one-man show *The Best of Times*, wherever we take it – from the Theatre Royal, Haymarket to Chichester and Regent's Park. Then a production of *In Praise of Rattigan* – scenes from many of his plays read by Dorothy Tutin, Paul Eddington, Christopher Cazenove and Judi Dench, which was enormously satisfying, especially as I'm sure it helped to revive interest in that wonderful playwright, whose work had fallen out of fashion for some years. Stella has now returned joyfully to radio work 'because I don't have to learn the lines'. She doesn't sit around twiddling her thumbs.

In 1999, Trevor Nunn came up with Ensemble 99, a company within the existing National company – in some ways a more difficult trick to pull off than the one Peter Hall achieved two years before, casting his company from scratch. Ensemble 99 succeeded brilliantly: a dazzling company – Simon Russell Beale, Roger Allam, Jasper Britton, Oliver Cotton, Peter McEnery, Sara Kestelman, Patricia Hodge; and once again, a rich mixture of plays – *Troilus and Cressida*, Bernstein's *Candide* (in a brilliant new version by John Caird), and *Money* by Bulwer Lytton. *Candide* had me playing old Martin forty years after I had played young Candide in the West End premiere in 1959. Then, in the twenty-fifth anniversary season of the National I found myself playing Polonius to Simon Russell Beale's Hamlet, exactly a quarter of a century after playing Claudius with Albert Finney as Hamlet in the very first production in the very first season of the new National Theatre. I had been with the National, on and off, since the day it was born. I had moved on a whole generation – and I didn't feel a day older...

Russell Beale's Hamlet was the best I have ever seen since my 17-year-old encounter with John Gielgud's eye-and-ear-opening performance all those years ago. He was witty (he got more laughs than any other Hamlet – all legitimate), he was sweetly charming and self-deprecating, his diction, like Gielgud's, was impeccable, observing the rhythm of the poetry without over-stressing it and losing the meaning, and his death was deeply moving.

Deliberate overtones of *Hamlet* ran through Charlotte Jones's delightfully offbeat and imaginative comedy *Humble Boy*, and I found myself playing a sort of comedic Claudius figure having a rumbustious affair with Russell Beale's mother, played by (yes!) Diana Rigg (coupling number six).

This season was crowned by an absolutely sizzling production by

Trevor Nunn of Cole Porter's *Anything Goes*, a classic Broadway musical, with some of Cole Porter's best songs – 'I get a Kick out of You,' 'Friendship,' 'You're the Top,' 'Blow, Gabriel, Blow,' 'It's De-lovely,' and of course, 'Anything Goes'. The book, originally by P G Wodehouse and others, has been through several revisions and modernisations, but has kept the flavour of the original. It is corny, but has the great virtue of *knowing* it is corny; it implicitly says: 'We know this is an old joke, but you're still going to laugh at it.' It gave me one of the biggest and longest laughs I've ever had: Eli Whitney, a heroic drinker, is consoling his lady-friend Evangeline Harcourt over the loss of her little pet dog.

> ELI: (*Offering his hip-flask*) Here – have a snort.
> EVANGELINE: I've told you, Eli, liquor has never touched my lips.
> ELI: (*Awestruck*) You know a short cut?

Standing ovations are a rare event at the National Theatre – or indeed anywhere – but they happened every single night for *Anything Goes*, at the interval and again, even bigger and longer, at the end. As I write, this joyous, heart-lifting tonic is about to transfer to the Theatre Royal, Drury Lane.

Here are the headlines from the reviews by two of London's top critics of the recent production of Ibsen's *Brand*, starring Ralph Fiennes:

> 'FIENNES FIRE LIGHTS IBSEN GLOOM' (Charles Spencer)
>
> 'FIENNES FAILS TO IGNITE IBSEN'S RARE FIREBRAND' (Nicholas de Jongh)

And here are the extracts from two of the top opera critics on ENO's production of Prokoviev's *War and Peace*:

> 'THRILL OF BATTLE: Tim Albery's new production is massively educated and aware, bang up to the minute and a complete success. Principal casting is near ideal: Simon Keenlyside a natural for Andrew, Sandra Zeltzer looks and sounds gorgeous as Natasha.' (Rodney Milnes)

> 'COLD WAR DISAPPOINTS: Albery's uninspired direction reveals little theatrical energy and imagination. Simon Keenlyside's character remains frigid and remote, and Sandra Zeltzer doesn't possess the vocal or personal charisma to inspire devotion.' (Tom Sutcliffe)

And so to the Royal Opera House round the corner for *I Pagliacci*:

> 'The real star was the production. Franco Zeffirelli's latest warhorse lives up to the old boy's reputation... Watching an undeniably spectacular evening, it was hard not to feel... we shall not see its like again.' (David Mellor)

> 'Franco Zeffirelli, a poor confused old man... lost in showbiz. This jaw-droppingly awful half-evening is... a travesty of everything that opera should be about. Meretricious, castrated, de-natured, these clowns should go back to the circus where they seem to think they belong.' (Robert Thicknesse)

And here a couple of reactions to my performance in *Hamlet* at the National:

> 'Denis Quilley was a mellifluous unfunny Polonius.' (Michael Coveney)

> 'Denis Quilley is a wonderfully funny and unusually affectionate Polonius.' (Charles Spencer)

Well, either Ralph Fiennes lit that fire or he didn't, Tim Albery's production was either a complete success or it was uninspired, Zeffirelli is either the last great genius or a clapped-out old hack, and my Polonius was either unfunny or wonderfully funny – it couldn't have been both.

These contradictions are easy to find: I could have given you dozens more because they happen all the time – I would hazard a guess that hardly a major production goes by without at least one pair of critics offering diametrically opposite judgments every bit as blatant as those I have quoted. It is not a question of one of them catching a good performance and the other an off-night, because all the front-line critics are there on the same night and see exactly the same performance.

I draw attention to this strange state of affairs, not to say that one critic is right and another wrong, one good and another bad, but simply to point out (and it is probably perfectly obvious) how extraordinarily subjective this whole business is. These contradictions do not seem to emerge with anything like the same clarity in other fields of artistic activity, and I think I know why – at least I can make a guess. In the visual and plastic arts, for example, you look at a painting, a sculpture or a piece of pottery and essentially you are looking at an *object*, not at the creator or maker of that object. You are not watching the potter firing his kiln or the painter putting brush to canvas. In the case of a large sculpture you do not see the skilled craftsmen who labour to bring the sculptor's small maquette to full size and full life, rather as the actors labour to bring their author's printed page to life on the stage. The difference is that we do it in front of you – you watch us making the object.

This brings us, I think, to the crucial point. When you look at that artefact you are in contact with the *personality* of its maker only at second-hand, at one remove, through the medium of that object. In the theatre, on the other hand, the *personality* of the actor informs everything he does, and is put before you and involved with you throughout, even if he is playing a character completely different from himself. If you are not in tune with his personality you will not enjoy his performance; if you are, you probably will, even if objectively you can see things wrong with it. It is difficult to account for logically. You and I can sit side by side watching, let's say, Bruce Forsyth. I will say: 'Isn't he brilliant?' and you will say: 'Oh God, I can't *stand* him, he's my *least* favourite performer' – and there's not much either of us can do about it.

I think I am probably one critic's least favourite performer. I don't mind – everyone has to be *someone's* least favourite, and I know it is subjective – not just because other critics have disagreed with him, but because I *know*, objectively, that some of the performances he has hated were actually very good. And, like most actors, I know when I have given a bad performance. My Falstaff in *The Merry Wives* was only so-so (even though one critic said I played him 'as to the manner born'). My Helmer in *A Doll's House* at Nottingham was not very good, and there are a few others with which (at least in part) I have not been too pleased. On the whole, though, I think I can say I have kept up a fairly consistent and decently high standard. And I think I've earned some Brownie points for versatility: from *The Cherry Orchard* to *La Cage aux Folles*, from *Sweeney Todd* to *Privates on Parade*, from *Candide* to *The Tempest*, it covers a pretty wide range, and I must say I love jumping about from Shakespeare to a musical, from Ibsen to camp comedy: it certainly stops me getting into a rut.

In October 2000 there was an article in the *Guardian* newspaper by a Senior University Lecturer in Performing Arts which began: 'Of all art practices theatre alone has no purpose. It has lingered as long as it has through a class consciousness that places live performance above television and cinema as if the mere act of attending a theatre event provides some form of necessary cultural medicine.' It went on to say: 'mainstream theatre does not entertain' and 'theatre dialogue bears no relation to contemporary language' and '*Hamlet* is not and never will be of our time'. Therefore, it argued, all theatres should be demolished, or (I promise you) turned into snooker halls and massage parlours.

As I happened to read this in Dublin while touring in the National Theatre production of *Hamlet*, I was almost as amused as I was enraged. Obviously Shakespeare's language differs in some respects from the language of today – he was, after all, writing 400 years ago. Mozart did not compose in the same idiom as a post-Schoenberg atonalist – does this mean that *The Marriage of Figaro* 'is not and never will be of our time' and that the Festival Hall should be turned into a bingo hall?

Had the author of the article been present to see and hear the respectable matrons of Malvern, the rather more raffish denizens of Brighton, and the tough, streetwise young Glaswegians and Dubliners laughing delightedly at Simon Russell Beale's witty and endearing prince and whistling and roaring their approval at the final curtain every night, I fancy he might have had to revise his opinion that the theatre does not entertain. 'We get our narrative fix,' he writes, 'from *EastEnders*, films and *Big Brother*.' Any commercial TV station which offered a season of plays such as *King Lear* or *A Streetcar Named Desire*, he proclaims, would go broke. Indeed it would, because (although there are quite a few of us who enjoy both) the people who enjoy *EastEnders* vastly outnumber those who enjoy *King Lear*. This is neither a good thing nor a bad thing, merely a fact of life. The *Sun* newspaper has a readership many, many times greater than that of the *Guardian*. Does that make it a better newspaper? And should the *Guardian* therefore be closed down and its offices turned into a snooker hall?

Cinema and television produce some great art and a good deal of rubbish. So does the theatre – so does every other art form. There is good and bad music, good and bad painting, good and bad fish and chips, and it is not snobbish or elitist to prefer the good in each case, and to try to learn how to recognise it. Finally the article derides the whole idea of live performance by saying that 'there is nothing magical or special about being in the same room as the actors'.

Well, statisticians ('Whom I will trust as I will adders fang'd' – *Hamlet*, Act III Sc 4) assure us that more people go to the live theatre in London than go to football matches. As first sight this is so astonishing as to be unbelievable, but then one thinks: why do people go to a football match, especially one which they know they could watch on TV in the comfort of their own home? Why do fans go to a pop concert in a vast arena with a lousy view of the stage when they have all the songs on their CDs and can play them on their Walkman or watch the videos on MTV whenever they want? Why do people travel 12,000 miles to Sydney to see the Olympics when every event is beamed around the globe?

The ridiculously simple answer, of course, is: 'Because it is live!' People want to *be* there when David Beckham strokes that free kick into the net. They want to be there when Madonna struts her stuff in her pointy bra. They want to be there when Jonathan Edwards grabs the triple jump by the scruff of its neck. They want to share the same space with their heroes because there is not and never will be any substitute for watching a real live talented vulnerable human being at the very moment he is doing what he does best.

Just as faxes, e-mail or your mobile phone can never replace the simple but essential pleasure of actually taking your friend by the hand, looking him in the eye and telling him how happy you are to see him, so canned music, electronically transmitted pictures and computer-generated images can never replace the joy I feel when a thousand living breathing people sharing the same space with me, all laugh together, or go suddenly silent, or spontaneously applaud.

In this world of separation, computers and virtual reality there is no substitute for live theatre, be it drama or music. As actors we are taking part in a shared live experience every night, and that is why we do this job – we are sharing the words and music *with* the audience, and we give joyfully with our love, often (if we are lucky) receiving joy and love back from the people who've shared the evening with us.

That's what it's all about (Alfie). There *is* something magical and special about being in the same space as the actors – I've been there and I know. I must try not to be precious about this, but it really is an uplifting meeting of hearts and minds, and it is never quite the same from one night to the next. It is, like life itself, unpredictable, dangerous and beautiful.

The final paragraphs of this chapter have been edited from Denis' draft and original notes. SQ.

Envoi

LAST NIGHT STELLA and I went to see the new cast who have taken over in *Humble Boy*. They were very good – not as good as us, of *course*, but very good – and the play is as beautiful as ever.

Today we're having morning coffee in the kitchen. Jo is staying on the top floor until she can move into her new flat – it's over a fish and chip shop but has its own little back garden, which is something she has wanted for a long time. Sarah and Hayley are holidaying in Cyprus, Dave and Lara are downstairs with their two-year-old Jed and baby Rhys, who is exercising his powerful lungs (he might make a useful baritone one day) and Barney is slumped on the floor with his head on my feet and his eyes on the biscuit tin.

The slow movement of Rachmaninov's Second Symphony is playing on Classic FM, and Stella gets up with her eyes closed and dances slowly and ecstatically to the gorgeous, yearning music.

Fifty years fall away, and with my unread newspaper on my knee I sit and watch her, my eyes full of tears and my heart bursting with love.

Appendix
Denis Quilley on stage, film and TV

Stage work

MAN AND SUPERMAN (*Working as ASM*)	14/08/45	Birmingham Rep
SPRING GREEN (*Acting debut*)	11/09/45	Birmingham Rep
KING JOHN (*Robert Faulconbridge/Melun*)	1945/6	Birmingham Rep
THE LADY FROM THE SEA (*Lyngstrand*)	1945/6	Birmingham Rep
1066 AND ALL THAT (*Various*)	1945/6	Birmingham Rep

National Service 1946–48, Sudan Defence Force, Signal Regiment in Khartoum

THE LADY'S NOT FOR BURNING (*Richard; understudy first*)	1949/50	Globe
RED DRAGON (*Leading Seaman Kendall*)	1950	Phoenix
POINT OF DEPARTURE (*Mathias*)	01/11/50 26/12/50	Lyric Hammersmith trans Duke of York's Hippodrome, Golders Green
TWELFTH NIGHT (*Fabian*)	1950/1	Old Vic Co (Italy tour)
BLACK ARROW (*Richard Shelton*)	23/10/50 26/12/50	Arts Theatre, Cambridge Old Vic
MERCHANT OF VENICE (*Gratiano*)	15/01/51	Old Vic
AND SO TO BED (*Prodgers/Coachman*)	01/10/51 17/10/51 10/12/51	Leeds Grand New Theatre Strand
LADY WINDERMERE'S FAN (*Lord Darlington*)	15/09/52	Playhouse Nottingham
MAJOR BARBARA (*Bill Walker*)	29/09/52	Playhouse Nottingham
COLOMBE (*Julian*)	13/10/52	Playhouse Nottingham
FIGURE OF FUN (Bobosse) (*Freddie*)	10/11/52	Playhouse Nottingham
RUR (*Primus (robot)*)	24/11/52	Playhouse Nottingham
CINDERELLA (*Rudolf, Demon King*)	23/12/52	Playhouse Nottingham
THE TEMPEST (*Antonio*)	19/01/53	Playhouse Nottingham
A DOLL'S HOUSE (*Torvald Helmer*)	02/02/53	Playhouse Nottingham
AIRS ON A SHOESTRING (>700 perfs) (*Various/revue*)	23/03/53	Theatre Royal, Brighton Royal Court

WILD THYME *(Geoff Morris (1st lead))*	14/07/55	Duke of York's
A GIRL CALLED JO *(Laurie)*	15/12/55	Piccadilly
THE EAGLE HAS TWO HEADS *(Stanislas)*	21/05/56	Theatre Royal, Windsor
COME LIVE WITH ME *(Young composer)*	16/07/56	Theatre Royal, Windsor
GRAB ME A GONDOLA (>600 perfs) *(Tom Wilson)*	30/10/56 27/11/56 26/12/56 21/07/58	Theatre Royal, Windsor Lyric Hammersmith Lyric Hippodrome, Golders Green
CAPT BRASSBAND'S CONVERSION (3 wks) *(Capt Brassband)*	08/09/58	Bristol Old Vic
AS YOU LIKE IT *(Orlando)*	Nov 1958	Bristol Old Vic
CANDIDE *(Candide)*	Apr 1959 30/04/59	Oxford Saville
BACHELOR FLAT *(Mike Polaski)*	15/11/59	Richmond
UPPER CRUST AND CHIPS (2 wks) *(Conn Daly)*	01/02/60	Theatre Royal, Windsor
BACHELOR FLAT (1 wk) *(1 wk)*	07/03/60 11/04/60 May 1960	Royal Opera House, Leicester Theatre Royal, Brighton Piccadilly
WILDEST DREAMS *(Mark Raven)*	Sep 1960	Everyman, Cheltenham
IRMA LA DOUCE *(Nestor-Le-Fripé)*	Nov 1960	Lyric Plymouth & Alvin Theatre NY
MUCH ADO ABOUT NOTHING *(Benedick)*	10/06/63	Open Air, Regents Park
THE BOYS FROM SYRACUSE *(Antipholus of Ephesus)*	02/11/63	Drury Lane
HIGH SPIRITS *(Charles Condomine)*	20/10/64 03/11/64	Palace Manchester Savoy
THE LADY'S NOT FOR BURNING (2 wks) *(Thomas Mendip)*	15/11/65	Theatre Royal, Windsor
ROBERT AND ELIZABETH *(Robert Browning)*	Apr 1966	Australian Tour
THE ENTERTAINER *(Archie Rice)*	19/02/69	Nottingham Playhouse
THE RESISTIBLE RISE OF ARTURO UI *(Roma)*	02/04/69	Nottingham Playhouse
THE ENTERTAINER *(Archie Rice)*	22/09/69	Theatre Royal, Windsor
A DOLL'S HOUSE *(Krogstad)*	Jan 1970	Brighton (Uni of Sussex)
SING A RUDE SONG *(Alec Hurley)*	18/02/70 26/05/70	Greenwich trans Garrick
CORIOLANUS *(Aufidius)*	02/03/71	NT
THE CAPTAIN OF KOPENICK *(Superintendent/General)*	09/03/71	NT
TYGER *(Scofield)*	20/07/71	NT (New)

LONG DAY'S JOURNEY INTO NIGHT (*Jamie*)	21/12/71	NT (New)
RICHARD II (*Henry Bolingbroke*)	29/03/72	NT
THE SCHOOL FOR SCANDAL (*Crabtree*)	11/05/72	NT
THE FRONT PAGE (*Hildy Johnson*)	06/07/72	NT
MACBETH (*Banquo; then Macbeth*)	09/11/72	NT
THE CHERRY ORCHARD (*Yermolay Lopakhin*)	24/05/73	NT
SATURDAY, SUNDAY, MONDAY (*Luigi Ianniello*)	31/10/73	NT
THE PARTY (*Andrew Ford*)	20/12/73	NT
THE TEMPEST (*Caliban*)	05/04/74	NT
MAN AND SUPERMAN (5 wks) (*John (Jack) Tanner*)	05/08/75	Yvonne Arnaud, Guildford
HAMLET (*Claudius/Ghost*)	10/12/75 16/03/76	Old Vic NT, Lyttlelton
TROILUS AND CRESSIDA (*Hector*)	Jun 76	Young Vic Co
WARREN HASTINGS (*Warren Hastings*)	19/07/76	CFT Tent
TAMBURLAINE THE GREAT (*Bajazeth (Pt 1) Callapine (Pt 2)*)	04/10/76	NT, Olivier
CANDIDA (*Morell*)	23/06/77	Albery & Leeds Grand
PRIVATES ON PARADE (SWET award) (*Terri Dennis*)	17/02/77 02/02/78	Aldwych trans Piccadilly
DEATHTRAP (*Sidney Bruhl*)	26/10/78	Garrick
SWEENEY TODD (SWET award) (*Sweeney*)	02/07/80	Drury Lane
MACK AND MABEL (*Mack Sennett*)	16/09/81	Nottingham Playhouse
ANTONY AND CLEOPATRA (*Antony*)	19/05/85	Chichester Festival
FATAL ATTRACTION (*Gus Braden*)	26/11/85	Haymarket
LA CAGE AUX FOLLES (*Georges*)	07/05/86	Palladium
MY FAIR LADY (*Henry Higgins*)	19/01/88	ROH, Manchester Birmingham Hippodrome
HOUSE OF BLUE LEAVES (3½ wks) (*Artie Shaughnessy*)	20/10/88	Lilian Baylis
THE ROYAL HUNT OF THE SUN (*Francisco Pizarro*)	28/08/89	UK tour
THE SCHOOL FOR SCANDAL (*Sir Oliver Surface*)	24/04/90	NT, Olivier
THE WHITE DEVIL (*Brachiano*)	13/06/91	NT, Olivier
VENUS OBSERVED (*Herbert Reesbeck*)	20/05/92	Chichester Festival

SHE STOOPS TO CONQUER Dick Hardcastle	05/08/92	Chichester Festival
SWEENEY TODD (*Judge Turpin*)	02/06/93	NT, Cottesloe (& tour)
SWEENEY TODD (*Sweeney*)	16/12/93	NT, Lyttlelton
THE MERRY WIVES OF WINDSOR (*Falstaff*)	26/01/95	NT, Olivier
A PATRIOT FOR ME (*Baron Von Epp*)	13/10/95	RSC/Barbican
TWELFTH NIGHT (3 perfs) (*Sir Toby Belch*)	Mar 96	Barbados
THE TEMPEST (*Prospero*)	13/06/96	Open Air, Regent's Park
WASTE (*Cyril Horsham, MP*)	14/03/97	Old Vic
WAITING FOR GODOT (*Pozzo*)	27/06/97	Old Vic
KING LEAR (*Gloucester*)	24/09/97	Old Vic
RACING DEMON (*Bishop of Southwark*)	01/07/98	CFT
KATHERINE HOWARD (*Thomas Howard, Duke of Norfolk*)	09/09/98	CFT
BRIEF CANDLE (*Narrator/various*)	20/01/99	New End, Hampstead
TROILUS AND CRESSIDA (*Nestor*)	15/03/99	NT, Olivier
CANDIDE (*Baron/Martin*)	13/04/99	NT, Olivier
MONEY (*Sir John Vesey*)	03/06/99	NT, Olivier
HAMLET (*Polonius/Gravedigger*)	15/07/00	NT, Lyttlelton preview then tour
	05/09/00	NT opening night then tour
	11/06/01	NT, Olivier (17 perfs)
HUMBLE BOY (*George Pye*)	09/08/01	NT, Cottesloe
	24/01/02	Gielgud
ANYTHING GOES (*Eli Whitney*)	18/12/02	NT, Olivier

Select filmography

Where the Spies Are (1965); *Life at the Top* (1965); *Anne of the Thousand Days* (1969); *Murder on the Orient Express* (1974); *The Black Windmill* (1974); *In This House of Brede* (1975); *Masada* (1981); *Evil under the Sun* (1981); *Privates on Parade* (1982); *Memed My Hawk* (1984); *King David* (1985); *Foreign Body* (1986); *Mister Johnson* (1990); *A Dangerous Man – Lawrence After Arabia* (1991); *Storia di una Capinera* (1993).

Select TV work

The Merchant of Venice (1955); *The Desperate People* (1963); *Undermind* (1965); *Contrabandits* (1967–8); *Timeslip* (1970); *Long Day's Journey into Night* (1973); *Clayhanger* (1976); *The Serpent Son* (1979); *Honkeytonk Heroes – Rhinestone Cowboy* (1979); *The Crucible* (1981); *Number Ten* (1983); *Murder of a Moderate Man* (1985); *Anno Domini* (1986); *The Shell Seekers* (1989); *Cassidy* (1990); *Rich Tea and Sympathy* (1991); *Noel's House Party* (1992–7); *The Marriage of Figaro* (1994).

Index